Second Edition

THE LAW OF TRUSTEE INVESTMENTS

Christopher P. Cline

AMERICAN BAR ASSOCIATION

Real Property, Trust and Estate Law Section

Cover design by Andrew Alcala

Printed in the United States of America.

27 26 25 24 23   5 4 3 2 1

A catalog record for this book is available from the Library of Congress.

Contents

About the Author

Christopher P. Cline is the Senior Trust Advisor for Riverview Trust Company. He has over 30 years of experience working with high-net-worth families, including 17 years as a nationally recognized estate planning attorney. Chris works directly with clients to help them navigate the challenges of estate planning and trust administration. In particular, he assists clients with business succession, trust design, and charitable planning.

Chris spent the first 17 years of his career as a nationally recognized estate planning attorney, ultimately as a partner at Holland & Knight. From there he moved to Wells Fargo's Private Bank, where he spent eight years managing the Fiduciary Services team in Oregon and southwest Washington. In early 2016 he took the position of Chief Executive Officer at Riverview. In 2022, he moved to the Senior Trust Advisor role to focus on writing, speaking, and client service.

Chris is a fellow of the American College of Trust and Estate Counsel and nationally recognized speaker and author on numerous estate planning topics. He has written seven books on estate planning and has drafted trust and probate legislation for the state of Oregon. Chris is a former president of the Estate Planning Council of Portland and former chair of the Estate Planning and Administration Section of the Oregon State Bar and is currently editor of the Estate Planning and Administration Section Newsletter.

1

Introduction

Perhaps the most significant of trustee duties is the duty to prudently invest trust assets. This is true in part because trustee investing involves so many fundamental trustee duties: loyalty, impartiality, due care and diligence, carrying out the trust intent, and collecting and preserving assets. This duty has been codified in the Uniform Prudent Investor Act (UPIA), a version of which has been adopted in all but six states.[1]

A. Trustee Responsibilities

Both the trustee and the attorney have responsibilities under the UPIA. The trustee in particular has to master both the law and changing investment landscapes. First, the trustee must understand the nature of modern investments, which include not just publicly traded securities (stocks and bonds) and more difficult assets to manage, like real estate and closely held businesses, but also derivatives (like puts, calls, and options), insurance, and alternative investments such as hedge funds. Once the investments themselves are understood, the trustee must determine the tax consequences of those investments. In particular, the taxation of derivatives, of retirement plans, and of trusts themselves can have a significant impact on trust administration.

Once familiar with the types of investments available, the trustee must determine how investment theory impacts investment choices. For example, modern portfolio theory dictates that a trustee must address levels of diversification and risk in investment choices. Those choices also might be affected by the trustee's views about market efficiency versus behavioral finance, considerations of environmental issues, and active versus passive investing.

The decision about diversification, in particular, requires a great deal of trustee attention. For example, the trustee ordinarily has to review the assets she receives and determine whether they have to be sold. But there may be

1. Unif. Prudent Investor Act (Unif. L. Comm'n 1994), https://www.uniformlaws.org/committees/community-home?CommunityKey=58f87d0a-3617-4635-a2af-9a4d02d119c9.

circumstances that mandate that certain assets be retained (for example, when those assets have a special relationship to the settlor or the settlor's family). Case law in particular has significantly affected diversification requirements.

Another important factor affecting the trustee's investment choices is the language of the trust agreement. General investment principles can be overturned by the trust terms. However, terms that may at first blush seem clear have been interpreted in interesting ways by courts, leading to trustee liability in several cases.

In order to capture the trustee's investment decisions and communicate them effectively to the beneficiaries, the trustee must prepare a written investment statement, one that considers the entire range of trustee decisions: the beneficiaries' personal situations, the trust terms, the special circumstances surrounding the trust creation, the law of trust investments (including the case law), and the income and transfer tax consequences of those decisions.

Finally, once the investment choices have been made and the investment plan has been put into place, the trustee must monitor the portfolio on an ongoing basis and be ready to make changes to the distribution provisions if necessary, using tools available under local law.

B. Attorney Responsibilities

The trustee is not the only one with significant responsibilities; the attorney advising the trustee has a large role to play in trustee investments. This role is somewhat confusing, due to a central paradox: attorneys are not qualified to provide (and are not typically covered by errors and omissions insurance for providing) investment advice. However, attorneys are hired to interpret the law, one of which is the Prudent Investor Act. So the attorney, in the course of interpreting that law, comes dangerously close to providing such advice.

Like the trustee, the attorney must be aware of the various investment vehicles and the nuance of investment theory. The attorney must also understand the ways in which such nuance is blended into the law of investments, including the Restatement (Third) of Trusts and the Uniform Prudent Investor Act. The attorney also must be aware of all the possible contexts in which these laws can arise. For example, charitable remainder trusts and irrevocable life insurance trusts are both subject to UPIA rules, even though the investments in such trusts often are not considered in great detail.

The attorney also has to advise the trustee about her duties to the beneficiaries, which include the duties of impartiality and loyalty. Such duties arise in the investment context, particularly when the choice of investments can favor one beneficiary over another (for instance, in the case where one beneficiary is entitled to income and therefore favors investments in income-producing assets, and another beneficiary is entitled to the trust residue and therefore favors growth assets that produce little or no income).

The document itself is of course the attorney's area of specialty. In the drafting stage, the attorney must be aware of the kinds of issues the courts will examine when determining the extent to which trust investment provisions (and particularly those provisions that allow a trustee not to diversify) will be respected. The attorney also must know about the alternatives to traditional trust drafting, like total return trusts. These same issues are important when interpreting trust terms for a trustee after the trust has become irrevocable.

C. Who Should Use This Book?

This book was written with the individual trustee in mind. Corporate fiduciaries have all developed systems to take into account the issues raised here. However, the vast majority of trusts have individuals serving as trustees. These individuals are often either family members or trusted advisors (perhaps accountants or lawyers) who, although they may have adequate investment knowledge to manage their own affairs, will have little familiarity with the nuances of trustee investing. Further, the investment advisors whom those individual trustees have hired to manage the individual's personal finances also may not be familiar with these issues. So who should use this book?

- Individuals acting as trustees, who need to be aware of what they are about to get (or have already gotten) themselves into
- Financial planners who are used to advising individuals on their investing but who have little experience in the trust world
- Accountants who have been assisting individual trustees with their income tax issues and who have been called upon from time to time to give formal or informal investment advice
- Lawyers who draft trusts and represent trustees

It is this last group to whom this book is primarily addressed, because it is the lawyers who have perhaps the greatest potential liability exposure: they not only have the responsibility to ensure that the client's wishes are carried out by properly drafting the trust agreement, but they also are called upon by the individual trustee of that trust to advise on the responsibility of the trustee and of governing state trust laws.

2

Types of Investments

Defined broadly, trust "investments" include any assets held by a trust.[1] These can include, for example, personal assets such as furniture, furnishings and art, vehicles, vacation homes, and personal residences. None of these assets may be thought of by the trustee as "investments"; rather, they will be seen as something separate. However, when looking at the trust investments, a trustee must consider *all* of the trust assets, even those that are not managed by investment advisors.

The universe of investments can be broken down several ways: equity versus fixed income, publicly traded versus private investment, mutual funds versus exchange-traded funds, and so on. The division of asset type itself can be confusing. For purposes of this book, investments are broken down into five categories: (1) publicly traded securities (stocks, bonds, and cash equivalents); (2) real assets (real estate, closely held businesses, tangible personal property, and commodities); (3) alternative investments; (4) insurance; and (5) derivatives.

A. Publicly Traded Securities (Stocks, Bonds, and Cash Equivalents)

1. Stocks

Stock is an equity investment in a corporation. Stock can be common (which represents a simple ownership interest in the company) or preferred (which may guarantee a dividend but may represent a smaller equity ownership). Stocks can be publicly traded, in which case they are registered with the Securities and Exchange Commission, or the company can be owned privately, in which case the investment is made on the "private equity market." The pooling of money from wealthy investors, investment companies, and banks in this market is often referred to as "venture capital." When the company first goes public, it makes an

1. Unless otherwise noted, all definitions in this chapter are adapted from Kenneth M. Morris & Virginia B. Morris, Wall Street Journal Guide to Understanding Money & Investing (1999).

initial public offering, or IPO. If a company already has issued shares but wants to raise additional capital, the process is known as a "secondary offering."

Stocks can be divided not only between public and private companies but also by a company's size or market capitalization. A company with a capitalization of more than $10 billion is known as a "large-cap." These include companies that are on the Dow Jones Industrial Average (Dow) and the Standard & Poor's 500 Stock Index (S&P 500). A company with a capitalization of less than $10 billion but more than $2 billion is known as a "mid-cap." Mid-caps are included in some smaller indices and have a greater potential for growth than large-caps; however, there is also a greater risk of company failure. Finally, a company with a capitalization of less than $2 billion is known as a "small-cap." Small-caps have the greatest potential for gain but also for failure.

Information about individual companies is of interest if an investor seeks to purchase only that stock. However, if the investor wishes to check the performance of the market as a whole, various market indices track different sectors of the stock market. Perhaps the most famous is the Dow, which monitors 30 industrial companies. In addition to the Dow, there are the following indices: (1) NYSE Composite Index, which includes all stocks traded on the New York Stock Exchange; (2) the S&P 500, which includes a base of 500 stocks, made up of 400 industrial companies, 20 transportation companies, 40 utilities, and 40 financial companies; (3) the NASDAQ Composite Index, which tracks the stock traded through its system; (4) the Russell 2000, which follows the smallest two-thirds of the 3,000 largest U.S. companies; and (5) the Wilshire 5000, which includes nearly all stocks traded in U.S. markets. The S&P 500 is often considered the benchmark for large-stock investors. It is a weighted index in that it is calculated by giving greater weight to those stocks that exert a greater influence on the direction of the market because of their market value.

2. Bonds

Stocks represent the equity side of security investing; bonds represent the debt side. A bond is a loan that pays interest over a fixed term, which is why it is classified as a fixed-income security. The bond's interest rate is competitive with rates comparable to other bonds being issued at the same time.

There are many different types of bonds, identified by the entity that is doing the borrowing. Corporate bonds represent borrowing by private corporations. U.S. Treasury bonds represent borrowing by the federal government, and municipal bonds represent borrowing by states, cities, counties, and towns. In addition to having different borrowers, the term of a bond can vary as well. Short-term bonds usually mature within one year, intermediate-term bonds usually mature in two to 10 years, and long-term bonds generally mature 30 years or more after the date they are issued. When a bond is issued, it is sold at face value. After it is issued, however, bonds are traded in a secondary market, which means that they are bought and sold through brokers in the same way that stocks are.

A bond's interest rate never changes, even though other interest rates do. A bond that pays an interest rate that is higher than the current interest rate in the market as a whole will be a more valuable bond, while one with a lower interest rate will drop in value. A bond purchased at par upon issuance and held until maturity faces the risk of inflation eroding its value. The longer the maturity of the bond, the greater the risk that inflation will rise dramatically and reduce the value of the bond principal repayment at the end of the term. A bond that pays an interest rate higher than the rate of inflation outperforms inflation, while one that pays a lower rate does not.

This is not, however, the typical way in which bonds are handled. Most are not held by one investor from the date of issuance to the date of maturity. Rather, investors trade bonds in the secondary market, which leads to price fluctuations according to the interest rate the bond pays, the degree of certainty of repayment, and the overall economic conditions that influence interest rates (particularly the rate of inflation). Generally, when inflation is up, so are interest rates. If new bonds are being issued with interest rates higher than a bond in the secondary market, the older bond will sell at a discount below the par value. On the other hand, if an older bond has an interest rate higher than the rates being offered by current bonds, then it will sell at a premium over its par value.

If an investor buys a bond at par value and holds it until maturity, the greatest risk to that investment (apart from the failure of the company or municipality issuing the debt, known as "credit risk") is that inflation will rise and reduce the value of the money paid at maturity to the investor. On the other hand, a bond that pays more than the rate of inflation becomes a very good investment.

The quality of a bond (that is, the level of assurance that an investor will receive all of the interest payments due and principal at maturity) can be determined in part by rating services. Investment-grade bonds (those rated at least an A by either Moody's or Standard & Poor's) tend to be bonds that are at least of medium quality and are at least currently adequate. On the other hand, "junk bonds," which have the lowest rating of all bonds, present a greater-than-average chance that the issuer will fail to repay its debt. These investments were attractive, particularly in the 1980s, because the yields were significantly higher than those generated by investment-grade bonds.

There is a separate type of note of particular interest: government bonds. These come in two variations: those issued by state and local governments, known as municipal bonds, and those issued by the federal government, known as Treasury bonds. Both generate a lower yield than those issued by corporations; however, municipal bonds are exempt from state (and possibly local) tax if the bondholder lives in the state where the bond is issued. Municipal bonds also are exempt from federal taxation. The U.S. Treasury issues Treasury bonds, notes, and bills. Treasury bonds typically have 30-year terms and are also known as "long bonds." Treasury notes typically are issued in two, five, or ten-year terms. Finally, Treasury bills, also known as T-bills, are available in 13-, 26-, and 52-week terms. U.S. Treasury obligations are exempt from state and local but not federal taxation.

Other types of bonds include zero-coupon bonds, which pay no interest but rather pay a lump sum accrued at maturity. Such bonds are purchased at a discount from par value. There also can be different bonds defined by the assets that back them up. For example, collateralized mortgage obligations are backed by a pool of mortgages. Convertible bonds allow the investor to convert their asset from debt to equity in the company. Other types of bonds include Ginnie Maes (GNMAs), which are issued by the Government National Mortgage Association; Freddie Macs (FHLMC), which are issued by the Federal Home Loan Mortgage Corporation; and Fannie Maes (FNMAs), which are issued by the Federal National Mortgage Association. These bonds are hybrids, in the sense that they are mortgage-backed bonds but also are issued by government-sponsored corporations. Finally, there are U.S. Savings Bonds, which differ from other bonds in several important ways. First, they are not marketable. In other words, they can be redeemed for cash but cannot be sold to another investor. They also resemble zero-coupon bonds in that they are purchased at a discount and accumulate interest until they are worth par value at maturity.

3. Cash and Cash Equivalents

Cash and cash equivalents are perhaps the simplest investment class and generally include (1) paper currency and coins; (2) checking accounts; (3) savings accounts; (4) money market accounts; and (5) short-term, liquid investments with a maturity of three months or less at the time of purchase, such as U.S. Treasury bills and commercial paper. This asset class is not typically used as an investment per se but primarily as a "buffer," used to anticipate future cash-flow needs without having to sell other assets, potentially at a loss.

B. Real Assets

These assets include direct investments in real estate; publicly traded funds that invest in real estate (known as "real estate investment trusts," or REITs); tangible personal property, such as art and collectibles; and commodities, such as oil and minerals, precious metals, and agricultural products. Interests in closely held businesses also fall into this category. These assets are often described as "real" or "hard" assets because they are physical or tangible assets that have intrinsic value as opposed to intangible property that has a more subjective value.

These "real" assets can be a challenge to manage. Income-producing real estate may require rents to be collected, maintenance, improvements to be made, and so forth. Art and other collectibles trade in separate markets, which will require specialized investment skills. Investing in commodities requires a knowledge of the market for the commodity being purchased. Real estate and some commodities may have additional risks associated with them, such as environmental issues. Holding an ownership position in a closely held business, even if nonvoting, requires a familiarity with the business operations. For these reasons, investing in these assets can create challenges in a portfolio for an investor without the necessary specialized skills.

C. Alternative Investments

"Alternative investments" is a somewhat vague category. It includes (1) private placement debt, (2) managed futures, (3) venture capital, (4) private equity, and (5) hedge funds. While alternative investments have the potential to enhance the return on investment, and in some cases the diversification, of an investment portfolio, they have a higher risk profile because they are generally more complex, less liquid, and less transparent than traditional investments. Accordingly, alternative investments typically require a skilled investor with a higher-than-average risk profile.

This section will focus on venture capital, private equity, and hedge funds.[2] These are, in the author's experience, the three most common types of alternatives.

1. Venture Capital and Private Equity

Venture capital and private equity are similar in concept but different in scope. "Venture capital" funds are pools of money gathered from institutions and wealthy individuals that invest in young, small companies. They take significant risk in betting on new ideas, hoping to gain great rewards when those ideas become popular and the companies "go public." Venture capital is most closely associated in the public mind with the technology community in the Silicon Valley of California; however, it also can be found in any area where new businesses are being created with new ideas (the biotechnology community in Boston, for example).

Private equity funds also gather pools of money from institutions and wealthy individuals. But where venture capital focuses on startup businesses, private equity focuses on acquiring mature businesses or single divisions of larger corporations. Private equity funds tend to be larger than venture capital funds and often rely on borrowing to execute transactions. These funds tend to look for companies that are undervalued or have had business setbacks, or divisions of companies that do not seem to fit the parent company's larger mission.

---

2. The definitions in this section are adapted from Dave Kansas, The Wall Street Journal Complete Money & Investing Guidebook, ch. 8 (2005).

2. Hedge Funds

The term "hedge fund" describes an investment structure, not a philosophy; hedge funds are private, unregistered investment pools designed to take advantage of market inefficiencies. They can be used for many different strategies, but in general they are "positions that will profit in a market decline by providing an offset, or hedge, to losses incurred on investments in the portfolio that are exposed to the market."[3] In other words, hedge funds typically (though not always) are used as a small part of a portfolio to balance out the occasional market downturns in the stocks and fixed-income portions of the portfolio (which will typically be the major portion).

A full discussion of hedge funds is beyond the scope of this book. They should be used only by experienced investors who are comfortable with the way that they work and the purposes for which they should be used. They can be challenging: they can have complicated tax reporting, multiple layers of fees and expenses, potential lockups (that is, periods of time during which the investment cannot be sold), and periods of illiquidity.[4] Further, they traditionally have had minimum investment requirements.

The following are some typical hedge fund strategies:[5]

- fixed income arbitrage (offsetting long and short positions in similar fixed-income securities);
- statistical arbitrage (also known as "equity market-neutral") (offsetting long and short positions in equities, seeking a net portfolio exposure to equities of near zero);
- convertible arbitrage (taking a long security position and hedging the market risk by taking an offsetting position, often in different securities of the same issuer);
- merger (or risk) arbitrage (purchasing the stock of a company being acquired while selling short the stock of the acquiring company);
- distressed securities (selling short the stock of a company that is encountering significant business or financial difficulties);
- event-driven strategies (attempting to predict the outcome of a particular transaction, like a corporate bankruptcy or reorganization, and the optimal time to commit capital to it);
- macro investing (attempting to identify extreme valuations in a market and bet on the anticipated price movement in that market);
- sector strategies (a manager who combines expertise in and financial analysis of a particular industry to identify the best profit opportunities in that industry);

3. Joseph G. Nicholas, Investing in Hedge Funds 12–15 (rev. & updated ed. 2005).
4. *Id.* ch. 2.
5. For a discussion of these strategies, see *id.* at 59–78.

- equity hedge, or long/short equity (involving core holdings of stock, together with short positions in stock, stock markets, or stock market derivatives, to generate a positive return while protecting against a general market decline);
- emerging markets (involving the use of expertise about a particular emerging financial market, particularly those for which information is not readily available); or
- short selling (involving taking profits from a decline in the value of stocks).

These examples are illustrative only, and there are many variations on them. However, several points about hedge funds become clear from these general descriptions. First, they all involve a fund manager attempting to exploit a particular inefficiency in a market, which means that the success of the strategy depends upon the expertise of the management team.

Second, many of these strategies, standing alone, look a lot like market timing, which (as will be discussed in the coming chapters) is probably not a successful long-term strategy. This means that the primary use for a hedge fund in an overall portfolio strategy is to "smooth out" the portfolio return. For example, an investor whose portfolio consists largely of U.S. stocks might invest a small portion of that portfolio in an equity long/short hedge fund to reduce the impact on the overall portfolio of a decline in stock market values.

D. Life Insurance

Life insurance can be seen as a separate asset class or a different vehicle to hold securities. Life insurance has its own unique characteristics, most notably a death benefit. But cash-value policies also hold underlying investments. To begin any discussion of life insurance as an investment, it is important to understand how the various insurance products work. This, in turn, requires an understanding of the types of products available, the way that they are illustrated, and the expense structure behind them.[6]

There are a multitude of insurance products, each developed as the needs of the clients and the demands of the market have changed. And new products are emerging fast enough that any written summary is in danger of becoming quickly outdated.

1. Term Insurance

In its purest form, life insurance is simply the insurance company gambling on the insured's life. The company decides each year how much it must be paid for

6. For a more complete discussion of the types of insurance products on the market, see Gary Lee & Craig Wilkey, 827 T.M., Life Insurance: A Practical Guide for Evaluating Policies.

it to assume the risk that the insured will die in that year and that the company will then have to pay the stated death benefit to the insured's beneficiaries. The amount it must be paid, in the form of an annual premium, is determined based upon actuarial assumptions about the insured, including the insured's gender, age, personal habits (e.g., smoking and skydiving), and medical condition and history. For example, an insurance company will accept a small premium from a 25-year-old healthy nonsmoker with no family history of illness but may require a large one for a 98-year-old smoker. This kind of "pure" insurance is called "term insurance." Term insurance is used primarily to provide security for younger insureds (or for group insurance, with a large risk pool) because the premiums become prohibitively expensive as the insured gets older.

2. Whole Life

As an alternative to term insurance, the insured can buy "whole life insurance," the premiums for which consist of a term insurance component and an investment component. The annual premium for a whole life policy is typically significantly larger than that for a term policy with the same death benefit. The extra premium is added to an investment account regulated by the state insurance commissioner. This investment account grows over time and becomes a part of the death benefit that is paid. For example, if the cash value in the policy grows to $750,000 by the time the insured is age 50, the portion of the premium paid each year allocated to the term component of the policy gets smaller because now the company is insuring the insured's life for only $250,000. Because the value of the investment account increases over time, the premium never increases (as it does under term insurance) because the amount of the premium necessary for real insurance decreases. If the insured lives long enough, the cash value in the policy increases to the point where it equals the death benefit, at which point the insurance company simply gives the money to the insured. This usually happens at age 100. The owner of the policy can withdraw the cash value in the policy at any time or can borrow against it; however, if the policy has too little cash, it can lapse.

3. Universal Life

In response to the high interest rates of the late 1970s and early 1980s, the insurance companies developed "universal life insurance," which is similar to whole life insurance but provides flexibility in the amount of premium the policy owner pays. The policy owner can pay larger premiums in the early years of the policy and then lower premiums (or none at all) later. If the cash value in the universal life policy drops below a given level, however, the owner will have to pay additional premiums; otherwise, the policy will lapse.

With universal life, the policy holder gives up the certainty of a guaranteed premium in exchange for a lower current cost and more flexibility in paying premiums. However, if more money is ever needed inside the policy (because the interest crediting rate dropped or mortality costs increased), then more premiums would be due. If the additional premiums are not paid, the policy eventually lapses.

4. Variable Universal Life

A decade later, after the significant rise in value of the stock market, policy owners grew tired of having the cash values of their insurance policies invested in "safe" regulated investments approved by the insurance commissioner (typically bonds and government-backed mortgages). The insurance industry responded with "variable universal life insurance." Variable universal life is a universal life product, but the cash value of the policy can be invested in one of several investment packages offered by the insurance company. For example, the insurance company may offer mutual fund packages allowing investments 100 percent in stocks or 50 percent in stocks and 50 percent in bonds. The policy owner is limited to the investment packages offered by the insurance company, which typically have above-average costs. These higher costs may be offset, over time, by the fact that the growth of the assets inside the insurance policy occurs free of income tax liability. Note, however, that this investment flexibility can work both ways. If the policy owner invests primarily in equities and the stock market is doing well, the cash value will build in the policy faster than expected, which means that the future premiums can be much smaller. On the other hand, if the stock market drops in value significantly, the policy owner may have to pay significantly larger premiums than originally quoted.

5. Newer Products

As the market entered the new millennium, interest rates declined, and the "tech bubble" burst. Insurance buyers were tired of universal and variable universal life products, so insurers began to offer new products to meet investors' needs.[7]

a. No-Lapse Guarantee Universal Life

No-lapse guaranteed products (NLG) offer a guaranteed death benefit but little cash value. As a general rule, a traditional universal life policy lapses if the cash value is insufficient to cover that policy's ongoing charges for insurance and expenses. Conversely, NLGs stay in effect for the guaranteed period, usually

7. All references in this section are adapted from Melvin A. Warshaw & Joseph K. Bragdon, *Current Trends in Life Insurance Choices and Strategies*, 42 Est. Plan. J. (Mar. 2015).

the insured's life, if all premiums are timely paid, even if the cash value is insufficient. Initially attractive, NLGs became more expensive and harder to come by as interest rates stayed low and the levels of reserves insurance companies needed to retain got higher. Further, the lack of cash value inside an NLG policy limits the ability to convert this type of policy to a different type if the insured's planning objectives change.

b. Traditional Universal with Durational Guarantees

Durational guaranteed products marry the flexibility of traditional universal life with a "durational" guarantee, typically until life expectancy, and some cash value build-up. Durational guaranteed premiums are lower than NLG premiums because the durational guarantee requires the insurance companies to maintain less in reserve. The risk with durational guaranteed products is that future premiums could increase if the insured lives beyond his life expectancy. This type of policy would work best for middle-aged insureds who have adequate time to build cash value inside the policy, which would provide for flexibility if the insured's planning objectives change.

c. Private Placement

Sophisticated and wealthy investors sometimes use "private placement" insurance, which is a type of variable policy that allows investments in non-SEC-registered funds.[8] Private placement insurance is best suited for younger investors who have low risk aversion and are knowledgeable about investments.

d. Index Universal Life

Recently, the fastest-growing life insurance product is index universal life insurance (IUL). In an IUL policy, cash values are eligible to receive "indexed interest crediting," which uses an equity index, such as the S&P 500, to determine the interest rate credited to the policy, rather than a fixed interest rate. The return on the cash value is often capped at 10–12 percent in return for a guaranteed floor of 0–2 percent. IUL is less risky (but with less growth potential) than variable life but more risky (and with much more growth potential) than traditional universal life.

E. Derivatives

The Uniform Principal and Income Act defines a derivative, in the context of trust investments, as

8. For further discussion regarding private placement life insurance and annuities, see LESLIE GIORDANI & ROBERT CHESNER JR., 870 T.M., PRIVATE PLACEMENT LIFE INSURANCE AND ANNUITIES.

> a contract or financial instrument or a combination of contracts and financial instruments which gives a trust the right or obligation to participate in some or all changes in the price of tangible or intangible assets or group of assets, or changes in a rate, an index of prices or rates, or other market indicator for an asset or a group of assets.[9]

Derivatives include futures, forwards, swaps, and options. Derivatives are typically contract-based and can be devised for almost any investment objective, so long as another party can be found willing to assume obligations required to meet those objectives.[10] As a result, it is very hard to define specifically what constitutes a derivative. However, one common thread throughout all derivatives is their ability to allow the investor to gamble on the price swing of an equity, a commodity, or another investment without necessarily owning that equity or other investment. In light of this gambling effect, derivatives are almost never a good trustee investment (with the possible exception of collars, discussed later).

1. Options

Options are themselves derivatives, but they also can be the starting point for other, more sophisticated derivatives. An "equity option" is an option on shares of stocks or stock indices. Most are "exchange-traded options," meaning they are traded on one of the public stock exchanges. A "nonequity option" is any option that is not an equity option (which might include options on debt instruments, commodities, and so forth), while an index option has as its underlying instrument an index like the S&P 500.

2. Puts

A put holder, the party holding the underlying asset, has the right (not the obligation) to sell that asset at a specified strike price for a limited period of time, for which the holder pays a premium to the writer of the put. The holder buys the put, essentially, as insurance against a decrease in the value of the underlying asset, without realizing any gain on sale or losing voting or dividend rights. On the other hand, the writer of the put seeks to earn the premium income and is betting that the stock will not drop to the strike price. The writer's maximum profit is the amount of the premium, while its loss can be the amount of the strike price if the stock price drops to $0 at maturity.

---

9. Uniform Principal & Income Act § 414(a) (2000).

10. Unless otherwise noted, all definitions in this section are adapted from James B. Ellis, *The Basics of Derivatives for Trust and Estate Lawyers: Puts, Calls, Collars and Forwards*, 9 Cal. Tr. & Est. Q. 23 (2003).

3. Calls

A call is the reverse of a put. The holder of a call has the right (not the obligation) to *buy* the underlying asset at a specified strike price for a limited period. Whereas the holder of a put is worried about the underlying asset dropping in value, the holder of a call expects the asset to increase in value. The buyer's potential loss, on the other hand, is limited to the premium paid for the call. On exercise, the buyer pays the strike price to the seller (or writer) of the call. The seller must deliver either the underlying asset or cash equal to the difference between the strike price and the market price at the time the call is exercised.

There are two types of call options: covered (in which the seller of the call already holds the stock) and uncovered (or naked) (in which the seller does not own the underlying stock when selling the call). Whereas the holder of the call is betting on the stock increasing in value, the seller of a covered call increases its income from the sale of the call by selling its stock at the strike price. In exchange, the seller gives up the right to appreciation in the value of the stock above the strike price. On the other hand, the seller of a naked call does not own the underlying asset and does not want the call exercised because that would mean that the asset has increased in value and the seller must buy the asset at a price above the exercise price. In other words, the seller of a naked call is essentially gambling.

4. Collars

A collar is an option strategy that allows a holder of a particular asset (usually stock) to establish a "floor" value through a put and pay for that put by sacrificing some potential appreciation through a call. The holder essentially "brackets" the value of the stock. This can be beneficial to trustees who find themselves with large concentrations of low-basis stocks, for example. The trustee would like to diversify out of this large position, but selling the stock would result in considerable taxable capital gains. The collar prevents the value of the stock from falling too far, and the price paid for this protection is the limitation on potential gain from future stock appreciation.

F. Ways of Holding Investments

Any of these asset classes can be held by private investors (although some of the "unregistered" investments, often alternatives, can be used only by wealthy individuals). However, not all need to be purchased outright (e.g., only buying one stock or one bond). They can be acquired as funds of investments.

1. Mutual Funds

A mutual fund is a single investment that holds potentially hundreds of different securities. Such funds are monitored by either professional managers or representatives of a particular "index." Mutual funds are created by investment companies, brokerage houses, and banks. There are a huge number of different types of funds, each with its own investment objectives and programs. Most mutual funds are "open-end funds," which means that the fund sells as many shares as investors want to purchase. "Closed-end funds," on the other hand, raise money only once and offer only a fixed number of shares. Given this limited number of shares, the market for them fluctuates in response to investor demand.

Mutual funds can be (among other things) (1) equity funds, which invest primarily in stocks; (2) bond funds; or (3) money market funds. Bond funds and money market funds can be either taxable or tax free. Mutual funds can be designed to generate primarily income, primarily growth, or some combination of the two.

The return of a mutual fund can be affected by the costs incurred by that fund. These can include loads, or sales charges that are tacked on when an investor buys shares in the mutual fund. They are a percentage of the investment amount and can be charged upon purchase, upon sale, or throughout the period the fund is owned. Funds that do not carry such charges are known as no-load funds. Further, the investment managers who run the funds will charge commissions of their own. These costs are far lower for index funds, which do not require supervision and investment decisions by the managers.

2. Exchange-Traded Funds (ETFs)

Unlike stocks, mutual funds are priced only once a day, after the close of trading.[11] However, in 2003, regulators discovered that certain investors were taking advantage of this pricing model through a practice called late trading, whereby investors purchased interests after the close of the market at the closing price with knowledge of after-close developments. This trading scandal made another kind of fund, the ETF, more popular. ETFs are basically mutual funds that trade like stocks, so their price is reset throughout the day. Investors purchase ETFs on stock exchanges, rather than directly from the fund company. They typically focus on a specific index (e.g., S&P 500, the Russell 2000, and so on). Although they are more flexible than some mutual funds, they can be pricier if acquired through a broker and traded frequently because each trade generates a commission to the brokerage firm.

11. Descriptions in this section are adapted from KANSAS, *supra* note 2, at 149–51.

3

Economic Theory of Investments

This topic may seem hypertechnical (or even uninteresting), as well as outside the attorney's area of expertise. However, understanding the law of trust investments requires a general background in modern financial theory, which has been incorporated into the Restatement (Third) of Trusts: Prudent Investor Rule[1] (the Restatement) and, through it, into the UPIA.[2] The attorney who advises a trustee on the UPIA needs to be equipped with some background in basic investment theory, for example, when the subject of passive versus active investing or ESG investing is raised.

A. Modern Portfolio Theory: The Basics

What follows is a general introduction to modern portfolio theory, the general investment approach on which the UPIA is based.[3] It rests on three main principles: present value, opportunity cost of capital, and risk.

1. Calculation of Present Value

Present value calculations simply recognize the common-sense principle that a dollar received today has more value than a dollar received in the future because today's dollar can be invested.[4] Present value calculations allow for several determinations to be made: (1) the current value of a payment to be received in the

1. Restatement (Third) of Trusts (Am. L. Inst. 1992). Note that the Restatement (Third) of Trusts originally kept the section numbers (§§ 227–229) of the Restatement (Second) of Trusts but renumbered them as §§ 90–92 in the final version. All references to any sections in the Restatement (Third) of Trusts in the footnotes of this book will include the current and original section numbers.

2. Unif. Prudent Investor Act (Unif. L. Comm'n 1994). The website of the Uniform Law Commission (http://www.uniformlaws.org) provides the complete text of the Uniform Prudent Investor Act.

3. For an excellent overview of the topic, see Jonathan R. Macey, An Introduction to Modern Financial Theory (2d ed. 1998).

4. *Id.* at 3.

future; (2) the current value of a stream of payments; or (3) the amount that must be invested today to receive a certain sum at a future date. Further, these calculations require the application of a discount factor.

2. Opportunity Cost of Capital

The concept of opportunity cost recognizes that "every venture undertaken means that some alternative venture must be foregone."[5] In combination with the concept of present value, it can be deduced that investors should pursue any investment opportunities if the rate of return for the investment exceeds the opportunity cost of capital. When making these comparisons, investors should determine the discount factor by looking at the rate of return offered by investments that are comparable to the investment being considered. The discount rate is best understood as the cost to the investor of borrowing to finance the investment. When choosing a discount rate, risk must be considered; the riskier the project, the greater the discount rate (risk is discussed next).

3. Risk

Two investment projects with the same expected return can have dramatically different risk characteristics that might make one project preferable over the other. For some amount of additional return, an investor may be induced to take additional risk. This is known as the "risk premium," which can be determined by calculating the difference "between the return on a risky investment and the return on an identical investment with zero risk."[6] In general, therefore, investors should prefer investments with low volatility and would demand a risk premium to accept an investment with higher risk.[7]

B. Risk and Diversification

As a general matter, investors must be paid higher returns in exchange for accepting greater risks. In this context, risk is defined "as the variance among possible outcomes associated with a particular investment."[8] Variance (often expressed in terms of "standard deviations" along a familiar bell curve) can be calculated not just for a single investment but also for a portfolio of securities. Typically when doing so, historical variance is used to predict future variance.[9] It is important to note that most stocks have a variability higher than a market

5. *Id.* at 10.
6. *Id.* at 15–16.
7. *Id.* at 17.
8. *Id.*
9. *Id.* at 20.

portfolio as a whole.[10] This means that the riskiness of the market as a whole is not simply the average variability of the individual stocks in a portfolio because diversification reduces variability. In fact, diversification reduces variability significantly, and a relatively small amount of diversification can generate a significant variability reduction in a portfolio.[11] Diversification reduces risk because different investments react differently to the same information, which means that investment movements are "imperfectly correlated."[12] Gains in stock values, for instance, may offset losses in bonds at any particular moment. However, risk cannot be completely eliminated through diversification because some risk cannot be diversified away.

This leads to a critical distinction in the concept of risk. There actually are two types: firm-specific (or unsystematic) risk and market (or systematic) risk. Unsystematic risk includes threats to specific companies (such as labor troubles or natural disasters) or to classes of companies (such as cuts in the federal defense budget). Systematic risk includes all of those risks that plague all companies at the same time, such as inflation, an economic downturn, policy decisions by the Federal Reserve Board, or international unrest. Systematic risk cannot be avoided, regardless of diversification. Put another way, the only risk associated with holding a well-diversified portfolio is systematic risk.[13]

Systematic risk involves "quite subjective judgments that are essentially unavoidable in the process of asset management, addressing the appropriate degree of risk to be undertaken in pursuit of a higher or lower level of expected return from the trust portfolio."[14] The trustee must take into account several factors in deciding the appropriate level of systematic risk the trustee will assume. There is no "objective, general legal standard" to be applied for a given degree of risk because beneficiaries can be disserved by undue conservatism as well as by excessive risk-taking. One obvious example is the fact that, if the purpose for which a trust is created cannot "tolerate adverse outcomes in the short run," the trustee should not adopt "a high risk/reward strategy."[15]

As a result, investors need "a very good excuse for not holding a diversified portfolio, because investors who do not hold such portfolios are assuming risks that they could easily avoid through diversification"[16] and, therefore, should seek a portfolio with the lowest level of risk for the desired rate of return. An investor's portfolio also should be efficient, which means it is a portfolio "in which an investor would have to: (1) accept additional risk to obtain a higher return; and

10. *Id.* at 21.
11. *Id.*
12. *Id.*
13. *Id.*
14. Restatement (Third) of Trusts, *supra* note 1, § 90 cmt. g [1992 § 227 cmt. g].
15. *Id.*
16. *Id.*

(2) give up returns to reduce the riskiness of the portfolio."[17] Rational investors should want to hold only efficient portfolios; however, efficiency may vary based upon the investor's personal taste for risk.

C. Market Efficiency

An important theoretical concept for a trustee to understand when deciding how to invest trust assets or choosing an investment advisor is the concept of market efficiency. The Efficient Capital Market Hypothesis (ECMH) posits that the price of a given security inherently reflects available information about that security at that point in time. If a market is efficient, then under ECMH, an investor cannot select a portfolio of securities that will consistently outperform that market. In other words, if markets are truly efficient, passive investing should be preferred. Whether or not that is true will be discussed later in this chapter.

Because the Restatement adopts, to some extent, the efficient market theory,[18] ECMH, and specifically the passive-versus-active question, is an important concept in building trustee investment portfolios.

D. Behavioral Finance and Investor Psychology

Since the 1990s, investment theory has been based on two principles: people make rational decisions, and people are unbiased in their predictions about the future.[19] Modern portfolio theory is built in part on these two principles. They are designed to provide insight in valuation, expected risk, and expected return.

However, many financial economists have concluded that investors are often irrational. "Behavioral finance," which now has its own Nobel laureates,[20] is the study of how emotions and cognitive biases affect financial decisions. This section will outline the nature of some of those biases and the impact they have on investors. Understanding these biases is important not just for providing investment advice but also for understanding why clients make certain estate-planning decisions.

As an initial matter, we are not always rational creatures. We all like to think that, if we just use our heads, there are few problems we cannot solve. However, research in the last ten years has shown that this may not be the case. Nobel Prize–winning economist Daniel Kahneman explains that our thought processes often can lead us astray.[21]

17. Macey, *supra* note 3, at 26 (citing Harry Markowitz, *Portfolio Selection*, 7 J. Fin. 77 (1952)).

18. Restatement, *supra* note 1, ch. 7, intro. at 6–7, reporter's nn. at 75–76.

19. John R. Nofsinger, The Psychology of Investing (4th ed. 2011).

20. See, for example, Richard H. Thaler, Misbehaving: The Making of Behavioral Economics (2015), for a discussion of the field's history.

21. Daniel Kahneman, Thinking, Fast and Slow (2011).

According to Kahneman, the central problem is that humans have two ways of thinking: System 1 (our fast, intuitive, and emotional sides) and System 2 (our analytical sides).[22] System 1 thinking occurs automatically and involuntarily: we see certain facial expressions and we know a person is angry; we see 2 + 2 and we know the answer is 4 (even if we try not to do math!); we see the letters "C-A-T" and we can't *not* read the word. On the other hand, System 2 is the way of thinking that allows us to determine the answer to 17 × 24. The first system requires no effort; it happens whether we want it to or not. This system, which helped our primitive ancestors quickly distinguish dangerous situations from harmless ones, operates all the time and continuously generates suggestions for System 2. Although System 1 generally is very good at what it does, it has its biases. Further, it cannot be turned off.

System 2, which is engaged when questions arise for which System 1 provides no answers, can be activated by a surprising event or when you are monitoring your own behavior. System 2 follows rules, compares objects on several attributes, and makes deliberate choices between options.[23] Unlike System 1, System 2 requires a great deal of effort and, therefore, is lazy. System 2 is typically in a comfortable low-effort mode, in which we engage only a fraction of its capacity. System 2 has trouble focusing on more than one thing, which can deplete its resources. For example, both self-control and cognitive efforts are System-2 efforts, and people who are simultaneously challenged by a demanding cognitive task and by a temptation are more likely to yield to the temptation.

These two systems, which ordinarily work well together, can occasionally conflict with each other. This occurs when we try not to stare at an oddly dressed person, force ourselves to read a boring book, and, perhaps most significantly, invest our money. We rely on "heuristics," or rules of thumb, developed by System 1, and our lazy System 2 does not intervene.

In the field of behavioral finance, investor behavior is often the product of heuristic-driven biases.[24] These biases can include representativeness (judgments based on stereotypes), overconfidence, conservatism (the inability to properly account for new information), aversion to ambiguity, and emotional and cognitive problems.[25] Heuristic bias leads to "frame dependence," which takes into account such factors as loss aversion and regret for past decisions. Taken together, heuristic bias and frame dependence cause prices to stray from fundamental values, potentially for long periods of time, making markets inefficient.[26]

22. *Id.* at 20–21.

23. *Id.* at 36.

24. Hersh Shefrin, Beyond Greed and Fear 13 (2000). This book synthesizes the early work of several academics in the area of behavioral finance.

25. *Id.* ch. 2.

26. *Id.* at 42.

E. Market Timing

Intuitively, people are tempted by the idea that they can sell securities when prices are relatively high and then buy back those securities after their value has dropped (or "corrected"). This is commonly known as "market timing." The "common-sense" notion is that, when a recession appears imminent, the investor sells her securities, anticipating the market decline. Once the decline has happened, the investor buys back the securities she sold, thus avoiding the drop in value.

The evidence suggests that most people (including investment professionals) can't time the market profitably. Rather, the most important factor in navigating investment volatility is not timing the market but rather time *in* the market. Since 1980 the S&P 500 has had over 10,000 trading days. However, if you miss only a small fraction of the best days, the impact can be traumatic: an investor who missed only the 50 best days out of 10,000 would have missed 97 percent of the return.[27] Further, most of those "best days" in the market occurred very shortly after most of the worst days. What this means is that even if you were able to predict the top and the bottom of the market during a period of volatility, your portfolio would still suffer below-average returns if your predictions or your execution was off by only a day or two.

In other words, the issue with trying to profit from market timing is not whether an investor can spot the coming downturn or recovery, but whether they can do so by pinpointing the actual days they occur.

F. Asset Allocation

The investment world has changed significantly over the past 30 years: "The number and variety of investment alternatives has increased dramatically, and the once well-defined boundaries between asset classes often overlap."[28] As a result, the importance of asset allocation has grown to become the "main work of the fiduciary investor."[29]

Designing an investment portfolio in this environment consists of the following four steps:

1. deciding which asset classes will be represented in the portfolio;
2. determining the percentage that each of these asset classes will be of the total;

---

27. Morningstar Hypothetical Growth of $10,000 invested in the S&P 500 Index (TR) from Jan. 1, 1980, to Dec. 31, 2021.

28. Roger C. Gibson, Asset Allocation: Balancing Financial Risk 11 (4th ed. 2008).

29. *Id.* (quoting John H. Langbein, *The Uniform Prudent Investor Act and the Future of Trust Investing*, 81 Iowa L. Rev. 641, 646 (1996)).

3. specifying for each asset class the range within which the allocation will be altered (to take advantage of relative performance among asset classes); and
4. finally selecting the specific investments within each asset class.

Following these steps, and thereby establishing a long-term investment policy, is what generates long-term returns, not moving in and out of investments. And, as mentioned previously, market timing does not work. For instance, it is much more important to forecast rising (or "bull") markets than downturning (or "bear") markets. The average return of an investor who correctly forecasts all the bear markets but only 50 percent of the bull markets will underperform a simple buy-and-hold strategy.[30]

Time horizon, on the other hand, is critical. There are two primary investment risks: volatility (i.e., the size of the swings up and down in value of a particular investment) and inflation (i.e., the general increase in price resulting in the decrease of purchasing power).[31] Each is affected differently by the passage of time. For example, the volatility found in equity investments swamps its expected payoff in the short run but makes it a clear winner over fixed-income investments in the long run. Inflation, on the other hand, may be an insignificant factor in the short term, but over time it can significantly erode the value of a portfolio (particularly one built primarily of fixed-income investments).[32] Interestingly, investors tend to underestimate their time horizon and, as a result, underweight their exposure to the more volatile investments that provide the best protection against inflation.[33] So determining the time horizon (for example, the life expectancy of the investor or trust beneficiary) can dramatically alter an investor's tolerance for volatility.

Once a time horizon is determined, the asset selection process can begin. The key in asset selection is diversification, which involves not only diversifying within an asset class (e.g., buying more than one stock) but also diversifying among asset classes (e.g., holding several asset classes in a portfolio). The benefit of this multiple asset class allocation is that it tends to yield greater returns with less volatility than one or two asset class portfolios.[34]

To summarize, the principles of investment management can be distilled down to addressing the two risks of volatility and inflation and avoiding the superficial allure of market timing. These risks are best addressed by determining the time horizon for the investment. Portfolios with short time horizons face danger primarily from volatility, while those with longer time horizons must seek to avoid loss due to inflation. Once time horizon is determined, a multiple

30. *Id.* at 78.
31. *Id.* at 89.
32. *Id.*
33. *Id.* at 101.
34. *See generally* Gibson, *supra* note 28, ch. 9.

asset class allocation may be the best way to implement an investment strategy designed to address that time horizon.

G. Active versus Passive Investing

As investors build a portfolio, they eventually have to address one of the most important questions in the investment industry: passive or active? The Restatement addresses the differences between "passive strategies" and "active strategies." Passive strategies involve investing in "index funds that track major stock exchanges or widely published listings of publicly traded stocks."[35] This is a "practical investment alternative to be considered by trustees seeking to include corporate equity in their portfolios" because it offers the "pricing security and economies of buying in essentially efficient markets."[36]

On the other hand, active strategies also are allowable, which involve hiring a professional to search for "advantageous segments of the market or for individual bargains in the form of under priced securities."[37] Such strategies, however, "entail investigation and analysis expenses and tend to increase general transaction costs, including capital gains taxation."[38] These considerations are "relevant to the trustee initially in deciding whether, to what extent, and in what manner to undertake an active investment strategy." If the costs and risks of such a program are substantial, they "must be justified by realistically evaluated return expectations."

Therefore, if the trustee decides to proceed with an active investment program, the trustee must make the determination that (1) gains from the program can reasonably be expected to compensate for its additional costs and risks; (2) the program is reasonable in terms of its economic rationale and its goal within the trust portfolio; and (3) the trustee has a credible basis for concluding that the asset manager has the competence necessary to carry out the program and that supervision of delegation, if any, is appropriate.[39] These comments comparing active versus passive strategies imply that passive strategies are the favored investment because there is no rigorous standard applied to such investments as there is to active ones.

But is it true that passive outperforms active management? To answer this question, you must first define your terms. First, what is "passive"? As previously defined, it would appear to apply primarily to the purchase of publicly traded stocks through low-cost "index" funds. But that, in turn, raises two further questions. First, how does it apply to other asset classes, like bonds, REITs, emerging

35. Restatement, *supra* note 1, § 90 cmt. h [1992 § 227 cmt. h].
36. *Id.*
37. *Id.*
38. *Id.*
39. *Id.*

market investments, and so on? Second, even for publicly traded stock, you have to decide which "index" you're talking about: the S&P 500, the Russell 3000, the Russell 2000, the Dow Jones Industrial Average? The question becomes even more complicated in the case of fixed-income investing. The Bloomberg Aggregate Bond Index (often referred to as "the Agg" and previously known as the "Barclay's Agg") is a broad-based fixed-income index that is often used by bond traders and fund managers either as the model for a bond index fund or as a benchmark against which a manager measures its performance. It consists of U.S. investment-grade fixed-income investments, including Treasury securities (which represent almost 40 percent of the total index), corporate bonds, mortgage-backed securities, asset-backed securities, and municipal bonds. It is one of the most (if not *the* most) commonly used total bond market indices.

But notice that, by definition, it does not include international bonds or high-yield (often known as "junk") bonds, both of which can be an important source of diversification. It also can be considered conservative, given its weighting toward U.S. Treasuries. In other words, "index investing" for fixed-income investments is not as simple or effective as it seems.

One investment consulting firm has evaluated the persistency of top-quartile mutual funds, both active and passive, since 2007.[40] This evaluation has consistently led to the observation that "actively-managed strategies tend to struggle in strong up markets compared to passive strategies, especially in domestic equity asset classes. Many asset classes generate outperformance in the top quartile of their peer group and to a lesser extent the median manager more often in down markets." Further, passive investing "does not completely insulate investors from volatility in relative performance compared to active peers and in some asset classes has guaranteed sub-par results over the most recent 10-year period."[41]

To conclude, the "active management versus index investing" debate is far from resolved. When the Restatement refers to index investing, it always refers to doing so with large-cap, domestic stocks. But even though such holdings may constitute the bulk of a trust portfolio, there are other corners of the market where active investment may still be justified.

H. Socially Responsible Investing

One aspect of investing that continues to draw attention is the extent to which environmental, social, and governance (ESG) factors should be considered in building an investment portfolio. Using such a perspective involves taking into account not only a company's profitability but also its impact on issues like climate change, labor conditions, board diversity, and executive compensation. The goal is that, by focusing on those issues, companies can be selected for portfolio

40. Fiducient Advisors, The Next Chapter in the Active versus Passive Debate (Sept. 2021).
41. *Id.*

investment that not only are generating a profit but also are better placed to be successful in the future.[42]

At its inception, ESG investing was referred to as socially responsible investing (or SRI). Early SRI investing relied on "negative screens," under which a portfolio manager would not invest in companies that the investor felt were ethically or morally wrong (such as oil, tobacco, or gun producers). Importantly, negative screening involves using a nonfinancial metric in determining whether or not to make an investment. In other words, it places a moral or ethical judgment on the part of the investor ahead of purely financial considerations. It was from this perspective that the comments to the UPIA, quoted earlier, put forth the view that social investing could violate a trustee's duty of loyalty. And in large part, this is the view of many lawyers and clients, despite the fact that ESG investment theory has developed significantly in the last 30 years.

A better way to think of ESG investing is as "ESG integration," a strategy that combines ESG factors (e.g., a company's environmental impacts, its labor relations, and how it interacts with communities) with traditional financial metrics when analyzing companies. The thought is that ESG integration improves stock selection by expanding the scope of information about a stock, thus identifying more potential risks and opportunities.[43] And indeed, studies have shown that funds using such an approach generate similar results to those that don't consider ESG factors.[44]

Such an analysis presumes, however, that stock selection is being used at all. Such is the case with actively managed funds, in which fund managers believe they can deliver higher returns through their analysis and selection of individual securities. However, passive investing, as just discussed, does not use any stock selection at all. As a result, its administrative costs (the salaries it pays to fund managers and analysts) are significantly lower.

Which raises the question whether ESG-integrated portfolios (which are by definition actively managed) outperform an appropriate passive index benchmark. At least one study found that, although ESG portfolios performed better, in general, than the fund universe as a whole (which would include active and passive funds), such portfolios will always be more expensive than their passive index-tracking counterparts.[45]

Another concern for ESG investing is the extent to which fund managers engage in "greenwashing"; that is, expressing concern for and taking superficial steps toward ESG factors simply as a cover to sell more investment products. One recent example involved a raid by the authorities on the Frankfurt office of Deutsche Bank AG and its asset-management subsidiary over allegations that

42. For an excellent discussion, see Susan N. Gary, *Best Interests in the Long Term: Fiduciary Duties and ESG Integration*, 90 U. Colo. L. Rev. 731 (2019).

43. *Id.* at 745–46.

44. *Id.*

45. *Id.* at 756.

they made unsupported claims about ESG investments.[46] Such unsupported claims are common; surveys of managers tend to show that 68–74 percent of them claim to use ESG integration, but these results are self-reported with no oversight. There are few standard definitions or assessments. At least one consultant has tried to apply due diligence to the process by asking whether the ESG integration is observable, material, and additive to the investment process. The consultant found that 86 percent of funds claimed to use ESG factors, but only 35 percent did so in a meaningful way, passing muster under the consultant's due diligence process.[47] Analysis like this shows how hard it can be to determine whether a fund has truly adopted ESG integration or has simply claimed to do so for window dressing.

46. *Deutsche Offices Raided over ESG Claims*, Wall St. J., June 1, 2022, at B11.

47. Fiducient Advisors, Greenwashing in ESG: Don't Judge a Book by Its Cover (Dec. 2021).

4

Income Taxation of Investments

When considering the return generated by a particular investment, the income tax consequences of that investment also must be considered. Different investments can generate tax at different rates, and some investments will generate no income tax liability at all. The following discussion provides only an overview of some of the federal income tax issues that can arise with trustee investments.

A. Ordinary Income Tax Rates

Internal Revenue Code section 1 imposes an income tax on citizens and resident aliens, which is computed by multiplying taxable income by specified rates. There are seven tax rates on ordinary income through the 2025 tax year: 10 percent, 12 percent, 22 percent, 24 percent, 32 percent, 35 percent, and 37 percent.[1] However, not all investment returns are subject to ordinary income tax rates. For example, an individual taxpayer's net capital gain is subject to five applicable capital gains rates (0 percent, 15 percent, 20 percent, 25 percent, and 28 percent), each of which applies to different types of capital gain.[2] These lower rates also can apply to "qualified dividend income," which includes dividends received during the taxable year from domestic corporations and qualified foreign corporations.[3]

Further, the Health Care and Education Reconciliation Act of 2010 (HCERA)[4] enacted section 1411, which imposes the unearned income Medicare

1. I.R.C. § 1(j)(2), added by the Tax Cuts and Jobs Act, Pub. L. No. 115-97, § 11001(a), effective for tax years beginning after December 31, 2017, and before January 1, 2026.

2. I.R.C. § 1(h). *See* ATRA, Pub. L. No. 112-240, § 102(b).

3. I.R.C. § 1(h)(11).

4. Pub. L. No. 111-152, § 1402(a)(1), (a)(4). Section 1411 does not apply to a trust if all of the trust's unexpired interests are devoted to section 170(c)(2)(B) purposes. *Id.* § 1411(e)(2). The section 1411 tax is subject to the estimated tax provisions. *Id.* § 6654(a), as amended by HCERA, Pub. L. No. 111-152, § 1402(a)(2), (a)(4).

contribution tax (often referred to as the "net investment income tax") on an estate's or trust's unearned income. This additional tax is 3.8 percent of the lesser of the trust's or estate's undistributed net investment income for the tax year or excess (if any) of section 67(e) adjusted gross income for the tax year over the dollar amount at which the highest section 1(j) tax bracket begins for the tax year.[5]

Finally, there are "recapture" rules that can affect the rate at which income is taxed. For example, "section 1250 gain" can result from depreciation recapture, while section 1231 causes recapture of ordinary income from gain recognized on the sale or exchange of property used in a trade or business.

B. Taxation of Derivatives

Derivatives have their own set of arcane tax rules. Here are a few examples:

- For the purchaser of an exchange-traded or over-the-counter option, the character of gain or loss is determined by the character of the property to which the option relates.[6]
- An investor holds a "straddle" if she holds two or more positions that offset each other. Section 1092 prohibits an investor from realizing losses on the disposition of less than all of the positions of a straddle to the extent that there is unrecognized gain at the end of the year in any of the offsetting positions.
- Certain short sales are subject to "constructive sale" rules, under which any gain is recognized as if the position were sold, assigned, or terminated at fair market value on the date of the constructive sale.[7]
- Under section 1256, certain contracts are treated as if they were sold for fair market value on the last day of each taxable year and then "marked to market" (that is, the basis in the contract is adjusted as if it were sold and with taxes paid taken into account).

The purpose of this brief discussion is to point out the complexity that derivatives can engender and the tax consequences they can generate. In the author's view, the complexity of both the investments and their tax consequences renders them inappropriate as trust investments for all but the most sophisticated investors and trustees.

5. HCERA § 1411(a)(2). *See* Treas. Reg. § 1.1411-3(a)(1)(ii), -3(e). For tax years through 2025, Congress modified the income tax brackets and rates and suspended miscellaneous itemized deductions. *See* I.R.C. §§ 1(j), 67(g), added by the TCJA, Pub. L. No. 115-97, §§ 11001, 11045, effective for tax years beginning after December 31, 2017, and before January 1, 2026.

6. HCERA § 1234(a).

7. HCERA § 1259.

C. Taxation of Retirement Plans and Individual Retirement Accounts

Another equally complex tax topic is the income taxation of qualified retirement plans and individual retirement accounts (IRAs). Income taxation of distributions from qualified retirement plans is governed by IRC section 402, while income taxation of distributions from IRAs is governed by section 408. Both of these sections provide that distributions are taxable to the distributee under section 72 unless an exception applies.[8] Further, death benefits under qualified plans and IRAs are "income in respect of a decedent" (IRD) under section 691.[9] Although this book will not provide a complete discussion of income in respect of a decedent, an individual who inherits items of IRD takes the decedent's basis.[10] In other words, distributions from qualified plans and IRAs are subject to income taxation, typically at ordinary income tax rates. This income tax liability cannot be avoided by beneficiaries who take such assets following the participant's death. This includes trusts that are named as beneficiaries.

Further adding to the complexity is the fact that "required minimum distributions" must be made from the plan (which generate an income tax liability) when the trustee of the trust is a beneficiary following the participant's death.[11]

D. Taxation of Trusts

Trustees must face an additional layer of income tax complexity when considering income tax consequences of investments; that is, the taxation of trusts. As with the rest of the material in this chapter, this discussion provides only an overview of the subject of trust income taxation.

As an initial matter, a trustee must determine whether the trust being administered is a "grantor trust." A grantor trust is any trust, or portion thereof, governed by IRC sections 671–679. If the grantor or another person is treated as the owner of any portion of a trust under sections 671–679, then that person's taxable income must include those items of income, deductions, and credits against the tax of the trust attributable to "that portion of the trust to the extent that such items would be taken into account under this chapter in computing taxable income or credits against the tax of an individual."[12] In other words, if a grantor or another person holds certain powers over a trust, as enumerated in those sections, then the items of trust income, deductions, and credits are treated as being attributable directly to that grantor or other person. In this circumstance, the trust can be ignored for income tax purposes. The powers that will cause a trust

8. Natalie B. Choate, Life and Death Planning for Retirement Benefits 121 (8th ed. 2019).

9. *Id.*

10. *Id.* at 308–09.

11. *See generally id.* ch. 1.

12. I.R.C. § 671.

to be treated as owned by the grantor include certain reversionary interests,[13] certain powers to control beneficial enjoyment of trust property,[14] certain administrative powers,[15] the power to revoke the trust,[16] and the ability to distribute income for the benefit of the grantor.[17] A person other than the grantor can be treated as the owner of the trust because of certain powers granted to him by the trust instrument and, therefore, can be subject to the taxation of trust assets. These powers include the power, solely exercisable by that person, to vest the trust corpus or income in himself or any powers described in sections 671–677.[18] Finally, there are special rules for foreign trusts having one or more U.S. beneficiaries.[19]

If the trust is not a grantor trust, then a different set of rules apply. Nongrantor trusts are a hybrid of an "entity" and a "conduit"; that is, some items of income and deduction are taxed to the trustee, while others are passed through the trust and taxed to the beneficiaries. The determination of whether items of income are taxed to the trustee or to the beneficiary turns on the concept of distributable net income (DNI). DNI is a quantitative measure of the income that the estate or trust can pass through to beneficiaries; it is also a qualitative measure of the character of income received by those beneficiaries. For instance, if a trustee holds as a trust investment municipal bonds that generate tax-exempt income, DNI will pass through to the beneficiaries the character of income received by the trustee, so the income may be tax-exempt to the beneficiary as well.

Additionally, and as mentioned earlier, the HCERA enacted section 1411, which imposes the additional 3.8 percent net investment income tax on an estate's or trust's unearned income. Section 1411 does not apply to a trust if all of the trust's unexpired interests are devoted to section 170(c)(2)(B) purposes.[20]

As a result of income tax reform, the income tax rate schedule for trusts was revised to eliminate any significant incentive to shift tax liability using trusts as separate entities.[21] The rate schedule for trusts reaches the maximum rate faster than the income tax rate schedule for individuals. Therefore, it is generally more advantageous for the trustee to pass income through to the beneficiary as DNI than it is for the trust to accumulate the income, potentially subjecting it to the highest income tax rates.

13. I.R.C. § 673.
14. I.R.C. § 674.
15. I.R.C. § 675.
16. I.R.C. § 676.
17. I.R.C. § 677.
18. I.R.C. § 678.
19. I.R.C. § 679.
20. For a more detailed discussion of the application of the net investment income tax to estates and trusts, see Jonathan G. Blattmachr, Mitchell M. Gans & Diana S.C. Zeydel, *Imposition of the 3.8% Medicare Tax on Estates and Trusts*, 40 Est. Plan. J. 3 (2013).
21. *See* I.R.C. § 1(j)(2)(E), added by the TCJA, Pub. L. No. 115-97, § 11001, effective for tax years before January 1, 2026.

E. Income Tax Definition of "Income"

With nongrantor trusts, income tax is paid by the trustee to the extent that income is retained; it is paid by the beneficiary to the extent it is distributed. Which leads to the next question: what is "income" in this context? First, the term "income," when not preceded by the words "taxable," "distributable net," "undistributed net," or "gross," means the amount of income of an estate or trust for the taxable year determined under the terms of the governing instrument and applicable local law.[22] DNI is a critical concept because, as mentioned earlier, it determines which portion of the trust or estate income is passed through to the beneficiary and taxed to him. It is the taxable income of an estate or trust with several modifications.[23] The most important of these modifications is the treatment of capital gains.

Internal Revenue Code section 643(a)(3) provides that gains from the sale or exchange of capital assets generally are excluded from DNI (and therefore taxed at the trust level) to the extent that these gains are allocated to trust principal. However, there is an exception for capital gains that are either paid, credited, or required to be distributed to a beneficiary during the year; or paid, permanently set aside, or to be used for charitable purposes. In these limited cases, even though the capital gains are allocated to principal, they are nevertheless included in DNI.

This can happen in two common situations: the trustee has the discretionary power to make distributions of principal, or the trustee is either adjusting between principal and income or distributing a unitrust amount following a statutory conversion. In both of these cases, the amount distributed does not depend upon how much capital gain is realized during a year, and it is difficult to ascertain whether proceeds from sale are actually paid to a beneficiary.

The Treasury Regulations provide, first, that "gains from the sale or exchange of capital assets are ordinarily excluded from [DNI] and are not ordinarily considered as paid, credited, or required to be distributed to any beneficiary."[24] There are, however, two exceptions to this general rule. The first, dealing with income of foreign trusts, will not be discussed. The second, however, provides that gains "from the sale or exchange of capital assets are included in [DNI] to the extent they are, pursuant to the terms of the governing instrument and applicable law, or pursuant to a reasonable and impartial exercise of discretion by the fiduciary (in accordance with a power granted to the fiduciary by applicable local law or by the governing instrument if not prohibited by local law)" in any of the three circumstances:

22. Treas. Reg. § 1.643(b)-1.
23. I.R.C. § 643(a).
24. Treas. Reg. § 1.643(a)-3(a).

- First, if they are allocated to income, with the proviso that if income under the state statute is defined as or consists of a unitrust amount, the discretionary power to allocate gains to income is exercised consistently and the amount so allocated is not greater than the excess of the unitrust amount over the amount of DNI determined without regard to this subparagraph (b).
- Second, if the gain is allocated to principal but treated consistently by the fiduciary on the books, records, and tax returns as part of a distribution to a beneficiary.
- Third, if the gain is allocated to principal but actually distributed to the beneficiary or used by the fiduciary in determining the amount that is distributed or required to be distributed to a beneficiary.[25]

Examples are provided in the regulations. First, the beneficiary has the right to all income and the trustee has the discretionary power to invade principal for the beneficiary's benefit and to deem discretionary distributions to be made from capital gains realized during the year. If during a given year the trustee has $10,000 of capital gain from the sale of securities, the trustee distributes $12,000 to the beneficiary pursuant to the discretionary principal distribution power, and the trustee does not exercise the discretionary power to deem that distribution as being paid from realized capital gains, then the gains are not included in DNI. Instead, the $10,000 of capital gain is taxed to the trustee at trust rates. More importantly, in the future the trustee must treat all discretionary distributions as not being made from any realized capital gains. This is part of the "consistency" requirement.[26]

In the next example, the facts are the same as in Example 1, except that the trustee intends to follow a regular practice "of treating discretionary distributions of principal as being paid first from any net capital gains realized by [the trustee] during the year." The trustee includes the $10,000 capital gain in DNI on the trust's federal income tax return so that it is taxed to the beneficiary. In future years, the trustee "must treat all discretionary distributions as being made first from any realized capital gains."[27] The third example provides a refinement of the second, where the trustee intends to follow a practice of treating discretionary principal distributions as being paid from gains realized from the sale only of certain specified assets or a particular class of investments. Such treatment is a "reasonable exercise of Trustee's discretion."

The next two examples discuss less likely alternatives. If the governing instrument, in a provision not prohibited by local law, allocates to income capital gains realized by the trustee, then those capital gains are includable in DNI for

25. Treas. Reg. § 1.643(a)-3(b).
26. Treas. Reg. § 1.643(a)-3(e), ex. 1.
27. Treas. Reg. § 1.643(a)-3(e), ex. 2.

the taxable year. Further, if the trustee decides that discretionary distributions are to be made only to the extent the trustee has realized capital gains during the year, then only $10,000, and not $12,000, would be distributable to the beneficiary in that year and all $10,000 is includable in DNI for that year.[28] Example 6 provides an unremarkable example of the treatment of proceeds of sale of real property where the proceeds are directed to be distributed to a specific beneficiary. Examples 7 through 10 all deal with different circumstances relating to the termination of a trust upon the beneficiary reaching a given age. Examples 9 and 10 are interesting because they address tax treatment for trusts that distribute half the corpus at one age and half at another.[29]

Examples 11 through 13 deal with distributions after the trustee has elected to pay an income beneficiary a unitrust amount. If the state statute provides that the unitrust amount is considered paid first from ordinary and tax-exempt income, then from net short-term capital gain, third from net long-term capital gain, and finally as a return of principal, and if the trust agreement follows state statute, then capital gains are allocated in accordance with the ordering rule and are includable in DNI to that extent.[30] If there are no such ordering rules, either in state statute or in the governing instrument, but rather such decisions are in the discretion of the trustee, and if the trustee intends to "follow a regular practice of treating principal, other than capital gain, as distributed to the beneficiary to the extent that the unitrust amount exceeds ordinary and tax exempt income then all capital gain is allocated to the trust and none is includable in DNI." Again, in future years the trustee "must consistently follow this treatment of not allocating realized capital gains to income."[31]

On the other hand, if under the same circumstances the trustee intends to "follow a regular practice of treating net capital gains as distributed to the beneficiary to the extent that unitrust amount exceeds the trust's ordinary and tax-exempt income and the trustee evidences this intent by including capital gain as DNI on the trust's income tax return then such a decision is a 'reasonable exercise of Trustee's discretion,'" and in future years, the trustee must "consistently treat realized capital gain, if any, as distributed to the beneficiary to the extent the unitrust amount exceeds ordinary and tax-exempt income."[32]

Finally, if a trustee (probably a corporate trustee) is acting as trustee of many different trusts, over which the trustee has elected to distribute to the income beneficiary a unitrust amount, and neither state statute nor any of the governing instruments of the trusts provide for an ordering rule, then the trustee may follow a regular practice of treating distributions from some trusts as coming

28. Treas. Reg. § 1.643(a)-3(e), exs. 4 & 5.
29. Treas. Reg. § 1.643(a)-3(e), exs. 6–10.
30. Treas. Reg. § 1.643(a)-3(e), ex. 11.
31. Treas. Reg. § 1.643(a)-3(e), ex. 12.
32. Treas. Reg. § 1.643(a)-3(e), ex. 13.

from capital gains to the extent the unitrust amount exceeds ordinary income while treating other trusts as though distributions are made from principal but not capital gains to the same extent, provided that the trustee treats each trust consistently in all subsequent years.[33]

33. Treas. Reg. § 1.643(a)-3(3), ex. 14.

5

Trustee Duties Generally

All trustees "are subject to common law duties and equitable rules or principles, which have been codified by statute in some instances. These fiduciary duties are fundamental to the trust relationship."[1] The famous general statement of the fiduciary duty is still Justice Cardozo's: "Many forms of conduct permissible in a workaday world for those acting at arm's length, are forbidden to those bound by fiduciary ties. A trustee is held to something stricter than the morals of the market place. Not honesty alone, but the punctilio of an honor the most sensitive, is then the standard of behavior."[2]

First and foremost, a trustee must "exercise the care, skill, prudence, and diligence of an ordinarily prudent person engaged in similar business affairs and with objectives similar to those of the trust in question." The question is not whether a trustee in any particular circumstance has acted reasonably or honestly but rather how that trustee's actions compare with the external standard of the ordinarily prudent and skillful person. This duty of care is "absolute, and the fact that the trustee was honest and well-intentioned will not excuse the trustee from a failure to exercise the required amount of diligence and prudence."[3] The standard is an objective one and is not dependent upon a particular trustee's skills or abilities. However, if a trustee has a higher degree of skill, that trustee will be expected to use that higher degree of skill and will be held to a higher standard.

This duty of care, sometimes referred to as the duty of prudence, actually includes a number of different responsibilities regarding the management and investment of trust property. For instance, a trustee managing a trust for multiple beneficiaries must follow the duty of impartiality, under which the trustee makes impartial consideration for the interests of all the beneficiaries, including not only the current or income beneficiaries but also remainder beneficiaries.[4] Trustees also carry a duty of loyalty, which is "the duty to administer the trust

1. Bogert's The Law of Trusts and Trustees § 541 (3d ed. 2021).
2. Meinhard v. Salmon, 249 N.Y. 458, 464 (1928).
3. Bogert's, *supra* note 1.
4. *Id.*

solely for the benefit of the beneficiaries and to exclude the interests of others as well as the trustee's own personal interest."[5]

A. Restatement Standard

The general duty of care with respect to trustee investing is set forth in the Restatement and the UPIA. The Restatement lays out five general investment principles:

> (1) sound diversification is fundamental to risk management and is therefore ordinarily required of trustees; (2) risk and return are so directly related that trustees have a duty to analyze and make conscious decisions concerning the levels of risk appropriate to the purposes, distribution requirements, and other circumstances of the trusts they administer; (3) trustees have a duty to avoid fees, transaction costs and other expenses that are not justified by needs and realistic objectives of the trust's investment program; (4) the fiduciary duty of impartiality requires a balancing of the elements of return between production of current income and the protection of purchasing power; and (5) trustees may have a duty as well as having the authority to delegate as prudent investors would.[6]

The Restatement incorporates the concept of risk discussed earlier,[7] distinguishing between systematic and unsystematic risk. The Restatement implies that a trustee may breach her fiduciary duty to preserve capital if she selects a level of return that allows inflation to erode the trust property's value. In other words, a trustee must accept a certain amount of systematic risk and avoid unsystematic risk by diversifying investments.[8] A trustee must "invest with a view both to the safety of the capital and to securing a reasonable return."[9] However, the goal of preserving the safety of capital includes both "the objective of protecting the trust property from the risk of loss of nominal value" and at the same time the "goal of preserving its real value—that is, seeking to avoid or reduce loss of the trust estate's purchasing power as a result of inflation."[10] Again, a trustee must seek an appropriate level of systematic risk, not avoid it completely.

The Restatement also adopts, to some extent, the efficient market theory.[11] Further, the Restatement specifically prohibits a trustee from incurring unreasonable costs in managing and investing trust assets.[12]

---

5. *Id.*
6. *Id.* § 90(c) [1992 § 227(c)].
7. *Id.* § 90 cmts. b, h [1992 § 227 cmts. (b), (h)].
8. *Id.* § 90 cmt. g [1992 § 227 cmt. g].
9. *Id.*
10. *Id.* § 90 cmt. e [1992 § 227 cmt. e].
11. *Id.* ch. 7, intro. at 6–7, reporter's nn. at 75–76.
12. *Id.* § 90 cmt. e [227(c)(3)].

Restatement section 227 states that the trustee "is under a duty . . . to invest and manage the funds of the trust as a prudent investor would, in light of the purposes, terms, distribution requirements, and other circumstances of the trust." This standard requires "the exercise of reasonable care, skill, and caution." Further, it is to be applied "to investments not in isolation but in the context of the trust portfolio and as part of an overall investment strategy, which should incorporate risk and return objectives reasonably suitable to the trust."[13]

B. Prudent Investor Act Standard

As indicated in its Prefatory Note, the UPIA is based on the Restatement. UPIA section 1 creates a "default rule," which "may be expanded, restricted or eliminated by the trust terms." Under section 2, a trustee "shall invest and manage trust assets as a prudent investor would, by considering the purposes, terms, distribution requirements, and other circumstances of the trust." Section 2(b) "sounds the main theme of modern investment practice," which is "sensitivity to the risk/return curve." This subsection "emphasizes the consolidated portfolio standard for evaluating investment decisions." An investment that, might be imprudent standing alone might be prudent if "undertaken in sensible relation to other trust assets, or to other non trust assets."[14] It follows the standard in Restatement section 227(a), which states that an investment "should incorporate risk and return objectives reasonably suitable to the trust." In other words, the apparently arcane concepts of investment theory discussed previously, and particularly the different types of risk, are very important to the investment decisions made by a trustee.

Under section 2(b), a trustee's investment choices are judged in the context of the trust portfolio as a whole and as a part of an overall strategy, after evaluating risk and return objectives. In other words, a trustee must develop an overall investment strategy. The comments point out, for example, that in a pass-through taxation regime "it may be prudent for the trust to buy lower yielding tax-exempt securities for high bracket taxpayers, whereas it would ordinarily be imprudent for the trustees of a charitable trust" to accept the lower yields generated by such assets.[15]

Section 2(c) sets forth circumstances that a trustee should consider in investing and managing trust assets, including general economic conditions, inflation, expected tax consequences, the beneficiaries' other resources, beneficiary needs for liquidity, and an asset's special relationship or special value, if any, to the trust purposes. Subsection 2(d) states that a trustee "shall make a reasonable effort to verify facts relevant to the investment and management of trust assets."

13. *Id.* § 90(a) [227(a)].

14. *Id.*

15. *Id.*

This duty of investigation includes the "traditional responsibility of a fiduciary investor to examine information likely to bear importantly on the value or the security of an investment—for example, audit reports or records of title." For example, in a California case, the trustees took on a junior mortgage on unimproved real estate. The trustees failed to have the land appraised and accepted an unaudited financial statement. In this situation, they were held liable for losses.[16] In general, subsections (a) through (d) impose a duty to monitor trust investments; "that is, the trustee's continuing responsibility for oversight of the suitability of investments already made as well as the trustee's decisions respecting new investments."[17]

Section 2(e) states that a trustee "may invest in any kind of property or type of investment consistent with the standards" of the Prudent Investor Act. This section "clarifies that no particular kind of property or type of investment is inherently imprudent."[18] Rather, the trustee has the responsibility "to invest at a risk level that is suitable to the purposes of the trust." Section 2(f) states that a trustee with special skills or expertise has a duty to use them.

This chapter having established a general sense of the trustee's responsibilities regarding asset management, the following chapters will address some specific trustee duties in more detail.

16. Estate of Collins, 72 Cal. App. 3d 663 (1977) (cited in Prudent Investor Act § 2 cmt. (1992)).
17. Prudent Investor Act § 2 cmt. (1992).
18. *Id.*

6

The Duty to Diversify

The most important aspect of a trustee's responsibilities with regard to investments is the duty to diversify. The issue of diversification (or nondiversification) has generated more litigation than any other aspect of the UPIA. There are, of course, times when diversification is not appropriate. However, the circumstances in which that decision is made involve many different issues.

A. Restatement Standard

Restatement section 227[1] provides that a trustee has a duty "to diversify the investments of the trust unless, under the circumstances, it is prudent not to do so."[2] A trustee, in investing trust assets, has a duty to the beneficiaries "to conform to any applicable statutory provisions governing investment by trustees" and also has the powers expressly or impliedly granted by the terms of the trust.[3]

The question often is raised by individuals acting as trustees whether they either should or must retain as trust investments those assets originally transferred by the grantor. Restatement section 229 places upon trustees the duty, "within a reasonable time after the creation of the trust, to review the contents of the trust estate and to implement decisions concerning the retention and disposition of original investments in order to conform to the requirements of §§ 227 and 228."[4] This duty requires the trustee, with the trust's investment objectives in mind, to "review the original investments, and, as necessary, formulate a plan for restructuring the portfolio to achieve a suitable level of risk and expected return with appropriate degrees of diversification and income productivity."[5] Further, the trustee's decision to retain or dispose of certain assets "may

1. References in the text of this chapter to section numbers in the Restatement (Third) of Trusts are to those originally promulgated in the Restatement (Second) of Trusts. The footnotes will include references to both the original sections and the renumbered sections.

2. Restatement (Third) of Trusts § 90(b) [1992 § 227(b)] (Am. L. Inst. 1992).

3. *Id.* § 91 [1992 § 228].

4. *Id.*

5. *Id.* § 92 [1992 § 229] cmts. 118–19.

properly be influenced, even without trust terms expressly bearing on the decision, by the property's special relationship to some objective of the settlor that may be inferred from the circumstances, or by some special interest or value the property may have as part of the trust estate." Examples of such properties include "land used in a family farming operation, the assets or shares of a family business, or stock holdings that represent or influence control of a closely or publicly-held corporation."[6]

The comments to section 229 provide two illustrations: In the first, a trustee who holds trust assets, 40 percent of which consist of shares in a single publicly traded corporation, is required to diversify the investments by selling a major portion of that stock. In the second, in which a trustee obtains a large farm as a trust asset and the trust (which terminates in a relatively short period of time) is established for the grantor's children, the facts are "sufficient to support a reasonable decision the trustee might make to preserve the farm assets and the opportunity they represent for [the children]," provided the decision is made with "care, skill and caution and with continuing consideration and reasonable balancing of the needs and potentially differing objectives of the individual beneficiaries."[7] Again, as noted, authorization to retain investments does not constitute an instruction to do so, and the trustee should not take a settlor's authorization to retain specific investments as special justification for retaining indefinitely investments that otherwise would be imprudent.[8]

The comments to Restatement section 227 describe the principles of diversification as well as some strategies for achieving it. Trustees should prefer to seek "the lowest level of risk and cost for a particular level of expected return." Diversification is "fundamental to the management of risk and is therefore a pervasive consideration in prudent investment management (indeed, to the extent practical, the duty to diversify ordinarily applies even within a portion of a trust portfolio that is limited to assets of a particular type or having special characteristics)." As a result, a fiduciary judgment is required that a trust, "in light of the amounts and timing of its cash needs and obligations, is in a position to accept the resulting risk of greater volatility in asset values, and therefore in portfolio performance for any given year or period." Finally, special circumstances may justify the departure from "an ordinary suitable diversified portfolio." Such departures may be justified by peculiar risks facing the beneficiaries' families, specialized investment capabilities, special interests or managerial abilities of the beneficiaries, or special settlor objectives (including particular asset holdings that are preferred or encouraged by the terms of the trust).[9]

---

6. *Id.* cmt. 119.
7. *Id.* cmts. 124–25.
8. *Id.* cmt. 125.
9. *Id.* § 227 cmts. 24–25.

The Restatement points out that asset allocation decisions "are a fundamental aspect of an investment strategy and a starting point in formulating a plan of diversification." These decisions "deal with the categories of investments to be included in a trust portfolio and the portions of the trust estate to be allocated to each." Such decisions are subject to adjustment from time to time, following changes in economic conditions or expectations. Basic classifications might begin with "cash equivalents, bonds, asset-backed securities, real estate, and corporate stocks, with both debt and equity categories further divided by their general risk/reward or income/growth characteristics, and by the domestic, foreign, tax-exempt, or other characteristics of the issuers and the like."[10]

For selecting a particular investment, the Restatement mentions five criteria: (1) expectations regarding the investment's total return, including the amount and regularity of the income portion of that return; (2) the degree and nature of risks associated with the investment and the relationship of its volatility to the diversification needs of the portfolio as a whole; (3) the investment's marketability, taking into account certainty of the trust's cash flow or distribution requirements; (4) transaction costs (including tax costs) and any special skills associated with acquiring or managing the investment; and (5) any special characteristics, such as exposure to tort liability, tax advantages and maturity dates, and possible redemption provisions of debt instruments.[11]

B. Prudent Investor Act Standard

Echoing the Restatement, section 3 of the UPIA states simply that a trustee shall diversify trust investments unless, because of special circumstances, the purposes of the trust are better served without diversifying. Such circumstances might include holding an undiversified block of low-basis securities that, if sold, would generate significant tax cost or retaining a family business.

Under section 4, a trustee has a duty, within a reasonable time after accepting the trusteeship, to review the trust assets and decide whether they are appropriate investments in light of the purposes, terms, and other circumstances of the trust and of the requirements of the Prudent Investor Act. In other words, a trustee cannot simply rely on the fact that her predecessor held these assets, even if her predecessor was the grantor. The comments note that, although the 1959 Restatement of Trusts took the view that "anytime within a year is reasonable," the 1992 Restatement retreated from this perspective, stating that no positive rule can be stated with respect to what constitutes a reasonable time for the sale or exchange of securities.[12]

10. *Id.* cmts. 25–26.
11. *Id.* at 43–44 (comments).
12. Unif. Prudent Investor Act § 4 cmt. (Unif. L. Comm'n 1994).

C. Case Law

As with all aspects of the law, statutes themselves can be difficult to understand until they are interpreted by reported decisions. The same is true for diversification standards for trustees.

1. Diversification Generally

In a paradigmatic case[13] decided before the UPIA was enacted, a decedent who was chairman of the board of the appellant bank created a trust, naming the bank as trustee and funding the trust primarily with the stock of the bank's own holding company. The beneficiaries argued that the bank breached its fiduciary duty to diversify and engaged in self-dealing by holding on to such a large concentration of its own stock. The bank argued that the terms of the trust modified the prudent person standard; the trust powers provided that the trustee had the power "to make new investments from time to time as it may deem necessary or desirable, regardless of any lack of diversification, risk or nonproductivity." The agreement also allowed the trustee to hold any assets originally received upon creation of the trust. The court, finding against the bank, held that the donor "did not intend to vest in the trustee Bank a power to diversify so little as to prejudice the interests of the beneficiaries."[14] The court also found that the bank "failed to provide a reasoned plan of investment calculated to accomplish the testator's purpose"[15] and that whatever plan it had was merely a justification for holding on to its own stock. This was due in part to the fact that the bank's own investment advisory service was recommending that no more than 5 percent of a portfolio consist of bank stocks.

The bank argued that even if a breach occurred, there were no damages because the trust suffered no loss. The court, however, held that although the value of the trust property had increased, the amount of the gain was much less than what would have been achieved through investment management. The beneficiaries argued that the appropriate measure of damages was the amount to which the trust property would have grown had the bank invested in a mix of the S&P 500 index and fixed-income Treasury bills. The bank argued that approach was speculative and done in mere hindsight. The court sided with the beneficiaries' witness and also awarded interest.

This case stands for two of the most important points of fiduciary investing. First, neither the trust drafter nor a trustee should rely on boilerplate language if the intent of the trustor is to allow the trustee to hold undiversified concentrations of any assets. As will be discussed later in greater detail, the drafter should include very specific language, worded very strongly, if this is the trustor's intent.

13. First Ala. Bank of Huntsville v. Spragins, 515 So. 2d 962 (1987).

14. *Id.* at 964.

15. *Id.*

A trustee, in the absence of such language, should seek either the consent of all the beneficiaries or instructions from the court authorizing an investment strategy that does not include diversification. Second, any investment strategy should be part of a plan that is well thought out from the beginning and communicated in some fashion to the beneficiaries.

A Washington case[16] reinforces the point that a trustee's duty of prudent investment is analyzed on the basis of the investment strategy, not on the overall return obtained by the trustee. Here, a decedent created a trust that paid income to her husband, with the remainder passing to her children after the husband's death. One significant trust asset was stock in a closely held company, which the husband sold for a large profit after the decedent's death. With this profit, the husband's overall return exceeded the total return that the corporate cotrustee would have obtained.

The husband argued that his performance should be evaluated based on that return. The court noted that, although overall trust performance "is a factor in evaluating the performance of the trustee," the husband "did not weigh his investment and income-producing securities against his investment in [the closely held corporation]. The overall trust performance was boosted dramatically by the sale of the [closely held stock] in 1983. But Mr. Cooper's investment strategy could not have anticipated the gain from the sale of the stock before it occurred." Furthermore, after the sale of the closely held stock, the husband invested "estate assets almost exclusively in marketable securities, 87% in bonds, favoring again the income beneficiary—him."[17]

An Ohio court,[18] however, reached a different result. There, the trustee held stock in The Limited, Inc., which grew from 11 percent of the trust's assets in 1981 to 66.6 percent of the trust's assets by February 1992. Although the trustee had a policy that a trust could not hold more than 10 percent of its assets in one stock, that policy was frustrated by the frequent stock splits. The beneficiary sued for failure to diversify, alleging that the bank's failure resulted in a significant decline in the value of the trust. The court, however, granted summary judgment in favor of the trustee bank on the grounds that the beneficiary failed to state any damages. It relied on the trustee's expert witness, who stated that the Limited stock overall performed more than twice as well as a similar investment in the S&P 500 and that, under the beneficiary's theory of recovery, pretax funds available for distribution would have been reduced from roughly $1.24 million to $362,000. The court relied on the Second Restatement of Trusts, not the Third Restatement or the Prudent Investor Act, so this case may be of limited usefulness.

---

16. *In re* Estate of Cooper, 81 Wash. App. 79 (1996).
17. *Id.* at 90.
18. Pickerel v. Huntington Nat'l Bank, No. 01AP-911, 2002 WL 416970 (Ohio Ct. App. Mar. 9, 2002).

In what seems a poorly reasoned decision, a federal district court[19] addressed a trust created in 1906 by the plaintiff's grandfather that began with a value of approximately $122,000 and grew to only $518,000. Another trust, created by the plaintiff's grandmother, was started in 1924 with approximately $149,000 but grew to a value of over $2,500,000. Upon learning of this "apparent disparity in rates of growth"[20] for the two trusts, the plaintiff filed an action against the corporate trustee for negligent administration of the grandfather's trust. The trustee moved to dismiss because the plaintiff could not demonstrate that the trust suffered a loss. The court found that, under Pennsylvania law, a beneficiary cannot prevail in a surcharge claim if she cannot show that there was a loss in the principal value of the trust. The court relied on a prior Pennsylvania decision that rejected the argument that a beneficiary suffers a loss because the return on trust investments did not keep pace with "certain stock market indicators."[21] This case is rather surprising; while it does not appear that the plaintiff provided much evidence of loss other than the disparity in return between the two trusts, the court did not look into the reasons for that disparity. For example, one explanation for the difference in values might have been that the trustee decided to invade principal more heavily for the plaintiff's mother (the current beneficiary) out of one trust than the other. Rather, the court seems to make the blanket assertion that, so long as the principal value of the trust increases, the beneficiaries cannot maintain an action against the trustee for improper investments.

2. Extent of the Duty

As will be discussed in Chapter 9, the Restatement and case law make it difficult for a grantor to override the duty to diversify. This raises the question of how far the duty extends and the circumstances under which it will or will not apply.

First, there is no absolute duty to diversify. In an Oklahoma appellate court case,[22] the settlors established a trust in 1957, funded primarily with stock in the AMP company. The trustee held the AMP stock as approximately 70–80 percent of the assets until 1998, when much of it was sold. Although the trust began with a value of approximately $75,000 and reached the value of approximately $514,591 in 1999, and approximately $600,000 was distributed over the life of the trust, the beneficiaries claimed that, had the trustee diversified, the trust's value would have been substantially higher. The trustee requested summary judgment on two theories: performance of the trust assets equaled or excelled the performance that conservative diversification would have produced and the trust instrument granted him wide discretion as to asset management. The court refused to uphold summary judgment on the basis of investment return because

19. Pitts v. First Union Nat'l Bank, 262 F. Supp. 593 (D. Md. 2003).
20. *Id.* at 595.
21. *Id.* at 597 (citing McCullough Trust, 21 Fiduc. Rep. 2d 135 (2001)).
22. Atwood v. Atwood, 25 P.3d 936, 940 (Okla. Ct. App. 2001).

the beneficiaries presented expert testimony to the contrary. However, while the court determined that the trust agreement provided no express exoneration, it ruled that the agreement granted the trustee the power to retain any assets for as long as he may deem advisable. The court rejected the beneficiaries' argument that whatever the trustee may deem "advisable" is subject to the Prudent Investor Rule and held that the Prudent Investor Rule did not create an absolute diversification requirement.[23]

In two other cases, courts have found that there is no absolute duty to diversify when such diversification is the result of bad trustee behavior. First, in *Brackett v. Tremaine*,[24] the trustee, a grandson of the settlor, sought to purchase for himself a 42-acre parcel of farmland that was by far the largest asset of the trust. The trust provided that the trustee was to receive income from the property for his lifetime and upon his death it was to be divided among the other beneficiaries. The trustee purchased a house and moved it onto the property before attempting to purchase it. He then petitioned the court for authority to sell, and the other beneficiaries objected. The trustee presented evidence from an expert witness that the greatest overall risk to the beneficiaries resulted from lack of diversification, which could be reduced by having a portion of the trust property invested in other assets. The other beneficiaries objected that the farmland was to remain in trust for all of the beneficiaries and that it would increase in value over time.

The court noted that the trustee had purely personal reasons for purchasing the property, and the trust agreement gave the trustee the power to retain any property "without regard to the proportion of such property or property of a similar character so held may bear to the entire amount of the trust."[25] Further, under the Nebraska Prudent Investor Act, one reason justifying nondiversification of trust assets is the asset's "special relationship or special value, if any, to the purposes of the trust or to one or more of the beneficiaries." Because the law "has looked with disfavor upon a trustee selling assets to himself," the court held that it "should not approve such a transaction over the objection of a beneficiary unless it can be clearly demonstrated that the transaction is consistent with the trustee's duty to administer the trust solely in the interests of the beneficiaries." The trustee could not meet this standard, so the court held against the trustee and against diversification.[26]

Next, a Pennsylvania court[27] held that, where a trustee exercised his power to diversify without regard to the actual facts, the diversification amounted to gross negligence. Here, a corporate trustee managed a trust, the purpose of which was to support the settlor's spouse, who was incapacitated and in ill health.

23. *Id.* at 945.
24. Brackett v. Tremaine, 269 Neb. 376 (2005).
25. *Id.* at 383.
26. *Id.* at 384.
27. *In re* Stella Scheidmantel, 2005 PA Super 6 (2005).

The largest single trust asset was stock in the corporate trustee. The trustee performed an "annual account investment review," after which it determined that the investment objective should be changed from "safety and income" to "balanced." Under this new investment objective, the trustee had the ability to allocate 50 to 70 percent of the trust assets to equities. Despite the fact that the income beneficiary's health was rapidly deteriorating at the time, the trust's "investment horizon," originally between three to seven years, was expanded to seven to ten years. Further, after the life income beneficiary's death and at a time when the trustee was required to distribute all assets to the beneficiaries, the corporate trustee actually purchased more mutual funds. Finally, the corporate trustee's investment advisor sold the corporate trustee's own stock immediately before dividends were issued, so that the trust assets did not include the additional stock generated as a result of that dividend. This investment advisor could not explain why he decided to lengthen the investment horizon.

The court first observed that Pennsylvania's Uniform Prudent Investor Act provision granted the trustee the ability to retain assets originally acquired from the settlor. The court then held that it was not attempting to "evaluate a trustee's management of trust assets with 20/20 hindsight, nor do we require a trustee to be clairvoyant in selecting only optimal investments that always appreciate in value and never decline in worth." However, even though the standard to which the trustee was being measured was that of gross negligence, the trustee "must be able to explain how an investment strategy was developed for a specific trust and why that strategy was prudent under existing circumstances . . . in other words, a trustee must be able to demonstrate that a chosen investment strategy was not based on a conscious, voluntary act or omission taken in reckless disregard of the consequences of the trust."[28] The corporate trustee "never consulted with the life tenant or the remaindermen" after taking over as portfolio manager. Nevertheless, it altered the trust's investment goal to "balanced" and increased horizon from "three to seven years" to "seven to ten years" even though it had no "factual basis for making these changes and [even though the trustee] never made any attempt to ascertain the Life Tenant's physical condition, his prognosis or his current income needs."[29]

In light of this, the court concluded that the trustee determined that "diversification of assets was a prudent course of action, as a general matter, without reference to the specific circumstances pertaining to" the trust. Finding, therefore, that the trustee had acted with gross negligence, the court stated that "diversification cannot become a goal in and of itself. Rather, diversification is a tool that can provide the means to effectuate a settlor's goals for a trust, if used properly and prudently with due regard to the specific facts and circumstances that exist in a particular case." Further, "[w]hether the method and mode chosen

28. *Id.* at 48.
29. *Id.* at 56–57.

for diversifying the assets of any given trust is [or was] 'prudent' or 'imprudent' necessarily must depend on the settlor's goal or goals in creating the trust and the factual circumstances surrounding the trust at the time a diversification program is initiated."[30]

A New York court[31] ruled that a corporate trustee holding a significant concentration of stock in a closely held business was not liable for its failure to diversify. In this case, the decedent, a daughter of the founder of a large manufacturing company (the Company), established multiple testamentary trusts at her death, each funded with large concentrations of Company stock. The Company is a closely held family business, the stock in which is not publicly traded. Each trust granted the trustee absolute discretion in managing trust assets and provided no instruction with respect to the Company stock. The trustees filed intermediate accountings, showing that the trustees retained Company stock. The beneficiaries objected, claiming that the trustees failed to adequately diversify the trust investments.

The court, finding in favor of the trustees, noted that the corporate trustee considered the liquidity (or lack thereof) of the Company and the fact that, because it was closely held, the trustees could obtain only a "speculative" price if it tried to sell the stock (this lack of marketability was exacerbated by the Company's unusual capital structure). The corporate trustee also considered general economic conditions, the adverse tax consequences of a sale of the stock, and the fact that the Company paid "considerable" dividends. Finally, there was an indication that the decedent wanted the Company stock to remain in the family and that the trusts were the vehicles chosen to achieve that result. In light of all these factors, the court held that the trustees were not liable for failing to diversify.

In *Donahue v. Donahue*,[32] the grantor established a family trust and funded the trust with $45 million in assets, which included an interest in an umbrella partnership REIT that constituted about 50 percent of the trust's assets. Following the death of the grantor, the grantor's brother, who was also the president and CEO of the REIT, was named trustee of the trust. In order to provide adequate income to the grantor's spouse during her lifetime and an appropriate remainder for the grantor's children, the trustee determined that he needed to diversify the trust assets because the REIT alone provided inadequate income. The trustee sold a 40 percent interest in the REIT and used the proceeds to pay off the family's mortgage on their residence, to fund trusts for the children, and to diversify in assets other than real estate. Three years later, the beneficiaries sued the trustee because the REIT had appreciated significantly in value after the sale, resulting in lost appreciation to the trust of approximately $20 million.

30. *Id.* at 59–60.
31. *In re* Hyde, 845 N.Y.S.2d 843 (2007).
32. Donahue v. Donahue, G040259 (Feb. 11, 2010) (unpublished opinion).

The court held that the trustee's diversification strategy did not violate the prudent investor rule. The beneficiaries argued that the trustee, as an insider, knew that the REIT interest would appreciate in value. Citing the housing crisis of 2008 and the collapse of Lehman Brothers, the court, however, found that the unreliability of long-term projections demonstrated the flawed nature of mere predictions of future performance, even those from financial advisors or insiders. The court reiterated that when executing the duty to diversify, the trustee is eliminating risks higher than suitable to a trust's purposes, return requirements, and other circumstances.

In an Illinois case,[33] the trustee breached his duty to diversify by retaining a 100 percent ownership interest in a family printing and newspaper business. The grantor created a trust to hold his ownership interest in a closely held business. In 1987, the trust appointed the Northern Trust Company as trustee. The trustee discussed at annual reviews the importance of diversifying the trust assets; however, the beneficiaries did not wish to sell the family business for various reasons. In 2000, the trustee assigned a new asset manager to the trust, who again stressed the importance of diversification. The trustee sought to sell a portion of the family business but, ultimately, determined that it was not in the best interests of the trust because many beneficiaries worked for the family business and a majority of the beneficiaries did not want to sell the business. The trustee did not perform any detailed analysis explaining the risk of not diversifying the trust assets. In 2007, the beneficiaries sued the trustee for failing to diversify the trust assets. The court held that the trustee breached his duty to diversify because the beneficiaries' requests to retain the family business and the trust instrument's instruction authorizing the trustee to retain the family business were not sufficient to exempt the trustee altogether from the duty to diversify. In other words, the beneficiaries argued that the trustee shouldn't have listened to them. The court agreed, finding a breach. However, it refused to hold the trustee liable for damages because the trustee's investments generated significantly greater income than the beneficiaries' hypothetical investment model.

Further complicating the problem is the breadth of investment options. Should a trustee of a trust that holds a single stock, for example, as its most significant asset be required to purchase a derivative (specifically, a "collar," discussed earlier) in order to avoid the swings in value that such a high concentration can provide? This issue has been raised in the context of individual investments, not trust assets, in a dispute that has spawned three separate decisions. While not arriving at a final decision, the U.S. District Court for the Southern District of New York allowed a case by an individual investor against a trust company to

33. Moss v. N. Trust Co., No. 7 CH 24749 (Ill. Cir. Ct. 2015).

survive summary judgment.[34] In this case, an individual investor hired the trust company to help him with the management of his assets, which consisted of a large block of stock in a single publicly traded corporation following the sale of his business. The individual could not trade the shares for one year after issuance. Because of this restriction, the individual alleged that the trust company told him that nothing could be done to diversify investments. However, the individual also alleged that, sometime after receiving this advice from the trust company, he was told by a broker that he could acquire a "collar" as a hedge against fluctuation in the price of this stock. He acted on this advice and purchased the collar, but only after the stock dropped in value. The individual sued the trust company, claiming that it failed to advise him about the availability of collars to avoid price fluctuations. The trust company filed a motion to dismiss for failure to state a claim; however, the court denied that motion. Subsequent to the issuance of the first decision in this matter, there were two further procedural decisions issued.

These decisions did not find that the trust company failed to advise the individual about the ability to "collar" his stock holdings and are of limited relevance to trustees, because they do not involve the trust company acting as a trustee. Therefore, the UPIA standards do not come into play. Finally, these cases involve a situation where the individual specifically asked the trust company for strategies to diversify. Nevertheless, they should stand as a warning to trustees who receive trust assets that are concentrated in a single stock. The trustee obviously must determine first whether the stock should be sold in order to diversify. However, even if diversification is found not to be appropriate (because of specific terms in the trust, because of adverse tax consequences upon sale, or for any other reason), the trustee should consider whether to take the next step of considering derivatives to protect against fluctuations in value. This will be particularly the case when the single asset is a publicly traded security, which can easily be hedged. This is not to say, of course, that all concentrated positions held by trustees should be hedged; for example, the purpose of the trust might be to hold the single investment because the grantor believes that the beneficiaries should benefit from that investment, and hedging would take away some (and perhaps a significant amount of) potential growth. Nevertheless, such a strategy should be considered by trustees facing this situation.

More recently, the Surrogate's Court of New York[35] held that an attorney-executor committed multiple, egregious violations against New York's Prudent Investor Act[36] by grossly mismanaging a decedent's estate, including breaching his duty to diversify. The executor knew that decedent's multimillion-dollar

34. Levy v. Bessemer Trust Co., No. 97 Civ. 1785, 1997 WL 431079 (S.D.N.Y. July 30, 1997); Levy v. Bessemer Trust Co., N.A., No. 97 Civ. 1785, 1999 WL 199027 (S.D.N.Y. Apr. 8, 1999); Levy v. Bessemer Trust Co., N.A., 2000 U.S. Dist. LEXIS 13275 (2000).

35. Matter of Kenney, 64 Misc. 3d 1232(A) (N.Y. Sur. Ct. 2019).

36. N.Y. Est. Powers & Trusts L. § 11-2.3 2019.

estate consisted of her home, checking and savings accounts, and General Electric (GE) stock that was not only the majority of decedent's investments but also the majority of decedent's entire estate. The executor failed to liquidate and diversify the estate's $4.6 million investment portfolio, 85 percent of which consisted of GE stock.

But failure to diversify was just the tip of the malfeasance iceberg. The executor did not maintain fiduciary standards when selling decedent's home. He failed to obtain a formal appraisal for the home, and he imprudently invested estate assets to renovate the property using a personal longtime contractor rather than selling the home in "as-is" condition. To make matters worse, the executor hired his personal contractor without soliciting other bids or entering into a written contract with a clearly defined scope of work. As a result, the house was sold at a total loss rather than at the lower "as-is" value he could have obtained. And of course, the executor paid himself legal fees for years without a court order, contrary to the requirement in the letters testamentary. The Surrogate's Court imposed numerous damages and surcharges due to attorney-executor's breach of his fiduciary duties along with statutory interest, denied him statutory commissions, denied him legal fees, and removed him as executor of the estate. This case is less instructive because the general breach of fiduciary duty was so broad, but it does point out that, during an estate or postmortem trust administration, an executor or a trustee should decide early on whether assets should be sold to avoid a drop in value. Here, "diversifying" probably really would have meant liquidating and going to cash or safe, short-term investments.

A Rhode Island case[37] supports the proposition that the extent of the duty to diversify depends upon the facts and circumstances of a particular matter. Upon the death of the grantor in 2010, a trust was created for the benefit of the beneficiary; however, the trust was to terminate upon the beneficiary reaching the age of 25, which would occur in 2014. The trustee had the discretion to distribute the trust assets outright to the beneficiary prior to 2014. When the trustee received the beneficiary's share of the grantor's estate in 2010, she placed the trust assets in a cash account. The trustee attempted to make an outright distribution to the beneficiary many times between 2010 and 2013. The beneficiary rarely responded to the trustee's letters sent by certified mail, telephone calls, and text messages. When the beneficiary did respond, she refused to sign a general release discharging the trustee of her duties and releasing her of any liability. This resulted in significant delays in, and additional expenses related to, the administration of the grantor's estate. The beneficiary sued the trustee for violating the prudent investor rule by placing the trust assets in a cash account that received less than $50 in interest income in four years.

The Supreme Court of Rhode Island held that the trustee did not violate her duties under the prudent investor rule by placing the trust assets in the cash

37. *In re* Bagdis, No. 15-40, 2016 BL 90944 (R.I. Mar. 24, 2016).

account because the trustee intended to make an outright distribution to the beneficiary and the beneficiary prevented the trustee from making the distribution for nearly four years. The court found the trustee's decision to place the trust assets in a cash account was reasonable to insulate the assets from the risk of market volatility, especially considering the short time horizon over which the trustee intended to hold the trust assets.

Similarly, in an unpublished opinion,[38] a California court addressed a trust, a cotrustee of which was also the trust accountant and who invested trust assets in Swiss bank accounts and fixed-income investments. The beneficiary became dissatisfied with the trust administration, including the trust investments. However, the court found for the cotrustee, finding that it was reasonable for that trustee to retain the majority of the assets in more conservative investments. Even though it found that "[t]he trustee has a general duty to diversify assets," the trustee did not breach this duty because the grantors were extremely risk averse, which justified the conservative investments. In addition, the investments produced sufficient income to cover the beneficiaries' expenses, and the court believed that investment in Swiss bank accounts was adequate diversification.[39] Thus, the grantors' intent to maintain a particular level of risk exposure helped to get the trustee off the hook.

Finally, even when a trustee tries to comply with the Prudent Investor Act, trustee communication with the beneficiaries (and internal communication, for corporate trustees) is still critical. A New York case[40] found that, where the investment officer assigned to a trust account sold concentrated holdings in order to diversify but did not tell the administrative officer in charge of the account the reasons for it, a triable issue of fact existed when a capital gains tax liability was incurred from the sale. There had previously been an understanding that the concentrated positions would be managed to avoid unnecessary sales. The beneficiary learned of this sale only when his accountant received a statement detailing his capital gains tax liability. Further, and more troubling for the court, the administrative officer did not know the factors that the investment officer considered at the time of the sale. Because this lack of communication created a triable issue of fact, the lower court's summary judgment in favor of the bank was overturned. In other words, even when a court might otherwise be inclined to relieve a trustee of liability, it may not do so if the trustee makes the right decision but does not communicate the reasons for making it.

---

38. Freedman v. Blumberg, No. B146760, 2002 WL 551021 (Cal. Ct. App. 2002) (unreported).

39. *Id.* at *3.

40. Margesson v. Bank of N.Y., 291 A.D.2d 694 (2002).

7

Duties of Loyalty and Impartiality

The duty to diversify, while greatly important, is not the only trustee duty with respect to investments. When choosing trust investments, a trustee must ensure that the trustee's decisions are in the interests solely of the beneficiaries and not of the trustee. Further, a trustee must act impartially toward all beneficiaries, even if those beneficiaries hold only a remainder interest (including those who are minors and unborn).

A. Restatement Standard

The trustee must "conform to fundamental fiduciary duties of loyalty and impartiality," and the trustee must "act with prudence in deciding whether and how to delegate authority and in the selection and supervision of agents." The trustee also must "incur only costs that are reasonable in amount and appropriate to the investment responsibilities of the trusteeship."[1]

The duty of impartiality derives from that of loyalty. However, the duty of impartiality can give rise to much more difficult issues. "Unlike the financial and other personal interests of the trustee, the divergent economic interests of trust beneficiaries give rise to conflicts of types that cannot simply be prohibited or avoided in the investment decisions of typical trusts."[2] This is because the interests of a life income beneficiary, for example, "are almost inherently in competition with those of the remainder beneficiaries, especially in light of the risks of inflation."[3] This conflict arises particularly when the income beneficiary is relying primarily, if not solely, upon the income (for trust accounting purposes) to make up for her distributions. If trust accounting income is the primary source of such distributions, then the income beneficiary obviously will want the trustee

1. Restatement (Third) of Trusts § 90(c) [1992 § 227(c)] (Am. L. Inst. 1992).
2. *Id.* § 90 cmt. c [1992 § 227 cmt. c].
3. *Id.*

to invest in those assets that generate as much trust accounting income as possible. Because these assets tend to generate very little capital appreciation, the remainder beneficiary will not want the trustee to pursue them. Rather, the remainder beneficiary would prefer investments in assets that appreciate in value but do not throw off significant amounts of income. As a result, these conflicting obligations "result in a necessarily flexible and somewhat indefinite duty of impartiality. The duty requires the trustee to balance the competing interests of differently situated beneficiaries in a fair and reasonable manner."[4]

Note that an income beneficiary "receiv[ing] principal in the trustee's discretion reduces but does not eliminate the productivity problem" (productivity here meaning the generation of trust accounting income). Wholly discretionary interests, on the other hand, with or without standards (such as "support") where the trustee's guidance "involve[s] distributive interests that do not distinguish between income and principal sources [. . .] therefore allow the trustee virtually to disregard income productivity in managing investments."[5] When a beneficiary is entitled to all of the trust income, "it is clear that the trustee has a duty to make the trust estate reasonably productive. But this does not make the character and extent of that duty clear." For instance, "the extent to which the needs, or any particular needs, of a life income beneficiary are relevant to the productivity objectives of a trustee's investment program is a question of interpretation."[6]

When dealing with this problem, the trustee "has a duty to consider two aspects of the productivity question." First, what is the appropriate level of productivity for the trust, and second, how should that productivity goal be incorporated into the overall portfolio strategy?[7] Note further that the power "to invade corpus is but one of a number of factors [a trustee] is to consider in weighing competing obligations and opportunities relevant to investment strategy." That invasion power "does not abrogate the duty of impartiality," however. For example, when the beneficiary of a trust is entitled to all of the income and a discretionary amount of principal as needed in the trustee's discretion for the beneficiary's support, that beneficiary is entitled to all of the net income of the trust, without regard to need. Therefore, the "investment authority of a trustee may not be exercised in a manner that simply disregards such a life beneficiary's potential interest in receiving income," even if the income distributed simply enhances the personal estate of that beneficiary.[8] It is possible for a trustee to intentionally pursue an underproductive investment strategy with the consent of the income beneficiaries who would be affected by this strategy; however, such consent must be fully informed and may be difficult to obtain.

---

4. *Id.*
5. *Id.*
6. *Id.*
7. *Id.*
8. *Id.* at 37.

B. Prudent Investor Act Standard

Sections 5 and 6 of the UPIA set out the trustee's duty of loyalty to the beneficiaries and of impartiality among the beneficiaries. The comments to the UPIA indicate that the duty of loyalty "is not limited to settings entailing self-dealing or conflict of interest in which the trustee would benefit personally from the trust." Rather, the trustee is under a duty not to be guided by the interest of "any third person."[9]

The duty of loyalty led the drafters of the UPIA to conclude that it could be breached by so-called social investing, for instance, if the investment activity "entails sacrificing the interests of trust beneficiaries—for example, by accepting below-market returns—in favor of the interests of the persons supposedly benefited by pursuing the particular social cause."[10] As discussed earlier, more recent developments in the area of ESG investing have rendered this viewpoint less relevant. However, the general proposition that a trustee cannot accept lower returns simply to put forward a trustee's nonfinancial agenda is still very relevant.

A trustee must invest trust assets solely for the benefit of the beneficiaries; transactions involving the trustee's own interests are generally prohibited unless certain standards are met. Breaches of this duty often occur when individual trustees invest trust assets in businesses in which the trustee has an (often controlling) interest and with corporate trustees who use their own proprietary funds.

C. Case Law

In *Jackson v. Mercantile Safe Deposit & Trust Co.*,[11] a corporate trustee was found liable for damages after failing to adequately monitor investments and investing in its own funds, which lagged behind the performance of the S&P 500. The corporate trustee assumed management responsibilities in 1947; by 1960, with a market value of $142,025, the trust assets consisted of a 70 percent stock/30 percent fixed income allocation. Annual reviews took place regularly, and until the mid-1970s the market value of the trust equities kept a reasonably close relationship to that of the S&P 500. However, in approximately 1975 through 2007, the S&P 500 returns significantly outpaced the trust returns. This resulted from three factors. First, the trustee sold the remaining stocks and bonds and invested almost exclusively in its own proprietary funds, which first occurred in 1975 and lasted until 1998, when the trustee determined that investment in its own funds might be contrary to the terms of the trust. Second, the trustee failed to maintain

9. Prudent Investor Act § 5 cmt. (Unif. Law Comm'n 1994).

10. *Id.*

11. Jackson v. Mercantile Safe Deposit & Trust Co., Civ. No. CCB-08-3048, 2012 BL 300343 (D. Md. Nov. 15, 2012).

any consistent balancing of the allocation of the trust assets. Third, there was frequent turnover of personnel handling the account; as it became a "smaller" account, it was passed to a less-experienced officer to manage. And, while the account in theory was subject to an annual review by the Trust Investment Committee, the records before the court did not reflect that such a review took place on any regular basis during the later years.[12] See also *Parris v. Regions Bank*,[13] in which a trustee's summary judgment motion was dismissed where trustee invested 72 percent of trust assets in trustee's proprietary junk bond fund, failed to disclose to the beneficiary material facts of the fund, and failed to diversify trust assets after the fund incurred significant losses.

On the other hand, in *Banks v. Northern Trust Corp.*,[14] the Ninth Circuit held that a corporate trustee that invested in its own funds did not breach its fiduciary duty. In this case, such investments were authorized by the trust agreement, they were permitted under state law, and beneficiaries received adequate notice.[15]

In a Pennsylvania decision, *In re Montgomery*,[16] the income beneficiary claimed that the asset allocation of 65 percent equities and 35 percent fixed income was not generating sufficient income. The court held that the portfolio balance was appropriate because it was designed to manage the trusts in a balanced and impartial way to meet the needs of the income beneficiary as well as grow the principal for the remainder beneficiary. The court observed that the allocation assured principal growth that benefits not only remainder beneficiaries but also the income beneficiary, as larger principal generated higher income from dividends, and that allocation of all trust assets to fixed income would result in a dramatic decrease in principal growth, while not gaining that much in the way of income. Note that this decision might have gone the other way in a higher-interest-rate environment; during the period at issue, stock dividends were close to bond yields.

In *Mennen v. Wilmington Trust Co.*,[17] the trust at issue held stock in the Mennen Company, which was privately held. Although Wilmington Trust Company was a named defendant, the trust agreement apparently named the individual cotrustee (who was also the brother of the trust beneficiary) as having sole investment responsibility. This may have been appropriate when the sole trust asset was stock in the family-owned business, but when that business was

12. *See also* Wagley v. JP Morgan Chase Bank, N.A., No. 18 Civ. 8668, 2020 BL 369314 (S.D.N.Y. Sept. 26, 2020) (court partially denied the trustee's motion to dismiss plaintiffs' breach of fiduciary claim where trustee engaged in "self-interested transactions" by investing trust property in proprietary funds directly managed by trustee).

13. Parris v. Regions Bank, No. 09-2462, 2011 U.S. Dist. LEXIS 92167 (W.D. Tenn. Aug. 17, 2011).

14. Banks v. N. Trust Corp., No. 20-55297, 2021 BL 296963 (9th Cir. Aug. 6, 2021).

15. *See also* Watkins v. PNC Bank, No. 2013-CA-001457-MR (Ky. Ct. App. Jan. 30, 2015).

16. *In re* Montgomery, No. 3007 EDA 2019, 2020 BL 307795 (Pa. Super. Ct. Aug. 13, 2020) (citing earlier decision *In re* Montgomery, 161 A.3d 392 (Pa. Super. Ct. 2017)).

17. Mennen v. Wilmington Trust Co., C.A. No. 8432-ML (Del. Ch. Apr. 24, 2015).

sold to Palmolive, suddenly the trustees had real investment work to do. The court presented the situation as follows:

> It is undisputed that the trust, once valued at over $100 million, was reduced to a value closer to $25 million through a series of debt and equity investments largely focused on two insolvent, unproven, and ultimately unsuccessful private companies with no established record of profitability. There can be no doubt that the investments were astonishing failures. The question is whether, divorced of hind-sight bias regarding the outcome of the challenged transactions, the trustees' investment decisions expose them to liability to the beneficiaries.[18]

The court found that the individual cotrustee used the assets of his brother's trust to further his own "pride":

> because most of the trustee's personal fortune was out-of-reach in his own trust, the trustee turned to his brother's trust as a piggy bank he readily opened to fund a few private companies in which the trustee had invested his time and on which he had staked a claim that he was uniquely skilled at selecting and advising small fledgling companies that he could turn into the "next big thing." Certain that fortune and acclaim were around the bend, the trustee eschewed the interests of the beneficiaries in favor of subsidizing his self-aggrandized standing as a financier.[19]

The individual cotrustee also failed to provide adequate investment information to his brother, overcharged on expenses, and was an unreliable witness. Therefore, the court had little trouble finding him liable, despite the presence of an exculpation clause in the trust. The court held that his actions amounted to bad faith, and therefore the clause did not protect him.

---

18. *Id.* at 2.
19. *Id.* at 3.

8

Power to Delegate and Duty to Monitor

Thirty years ago, trustees were largely unable to delegate their investment authority. This was not always as bad as it seemed, because most states significantly limited the types of investments a trustee could pursue. With the advent of the Restatement and the UPIA, trustees were given the duty to delegate many aspects of the investment responsibility. If done appropriately, the trustee would not be held liable for the decisions of the investment professional to whom the duty was delegated. However, the trustee is still responsible for hiring an appropriate and qualified investment advisor, for establishing an investment objective, and (most importantly) for monitoring on a regular basis the performance of that advisor.

A. Restatement Standard

The Restatement notes that delegation is not the same as abdication. A trustee "personally must define the trust's investment objectives." The trustee also must make decisions "that establish the trust's investment strategies and programs, at least to the extent of approving plans developed by agents or advisers."[1] The power to delegate arises particularly with larger trusts that invest in more technical or risky vehicles. For example, if the trustee intends to pursue a venture capital program, "the trustee[] would have not only the authority but a duty to delegate management activities in some reasonable fashion" if the trustee personally lacks the expertise and the time to manage such a program. Further, such delegation itself can be complex. In doing so, a trustee "must have, or obtain through the advice and assistance of others, the skill and time necessary to make a competent, careful evaluation of potential managers for the venture capital program and to monitor their performance of their duties."[2] The trustee also

1. Restatement (Third) of Trusts § 171, at 39 (Am. L. Inst. 1992).
2. *Id.* at 41.

must be able to develop "appropriate working arrangements and to negotiate an appropriate contract" with these managers.

B. Prudent Investor Act

Under UPIA section 9, a trustee who properly delegates investment and management functions is not liable for the decisions or actions of the agent to whom the function was delegated. A trustee properly complies with this section if the trustee delegates investment and management functions "that a prudent trustee of comparable skills could properly delegate under the circumstances." In reversing the former trust law that imposed a rule of nondelegation, section 9 "is designed to strike the appropriate balance between the advantages and the hazards of delegation." Further, the duty to minimize costs, summarized in section 7, applies to delegation as well. In deciding whether to delegate, "the trustee must balance the projected benefits against the likely costs." Additionally, "in deciding how to delegate, the trustee *must* take costs into account."[3] So, for example, if a trustee's regular compensation schedule assumes that the trustee will manage investments, "it should ordinarily follow that the trustee will lower its fee when delegating the investment function to an outside manager."

C. Case Law

In a Minnesota case,[4] the court held that the trustee properly relied upon the professional advice of a financial advisor in deciding the appropriate investment vehicles for a trust with an income beneficiary with special needs and remainder beneficiaries who were minor children. At the recommendation of the financial advisor and pursuant to a sophisticated investment plan, the trustee invested in three variable deferred annuities. The court found that the trustee, who had no prior experience managing trust assets, reasonably acted when she sought advice from the grantor's financial advisor. Even though the variable deferred annuities depreciated in value between 2007 and 2010, the court emphasized that the trustee obtained sufficient competent advice, guidance, and assistance to formulate and implement the investment strategy of the trust.

3. Unif. Prudent Investor Act § 7 (Unif. L. Comm'n 1994) (emphasis added).

4. *In re* Amendment & Restatement of Revocable Living Trust of Berget, No. A13-2295, 2014 BL 343076 (Minn. Ct. App. Dec. 8, 2014).

D. Duty to Monitor Investments

A case with serious consequences for trustees is *Tibble v. Edison International*,[5] decided by the U.S. Supreme Court in 2015. The facts are straightforward: the petitioners (beneficiaries of a defined-contribution plan) argued that the respondents (the employer and others, who sponsored the plan) violated their fiduciary duties by offering six higher-priced retail-class mutual funds as plan investments when materially identical lower-priced institutional-class mutual funds were available. The petitioners claimed that a large institutional investor could have obtained materially identical lower-priced institutional-class mutual funds that are not available to retail investors.

Ostensibly, the issue before the Court was whether the petitioners' claims were time barred under the six-year statute of limitations. The lower courts held that the statute began running when the mutual fund interests were acquired (eight years before the claim was filed), ruling against the petitioners' argument that, because the funds underwent significant changes within that six-year statutory period, the respondents should have undertaken a full due-diligence review at that time and converted the higher-priced retail-class mutual funds to lower-priced institutional-class mutual funds.

The Supreme Court overturned the lower court decisions, ruling that the petitioners' claims should be considered. The Court stated that in determining the contours of an ERISA fiduciary's duty, courts often must look to the law of trusts. It stated that "[u]nder trust law, a trustee has a continuing duty to monitor trust investments and remove imprudent ones. This continuing duty exists separate and apart from the trustee's duty to exercise prudence in selecting investments at the outset."[6] The trustee must systematically and regularly review all trust investments. The Court reached its conclusion based in part on the Uniform Prudent Investor Act. As a result, the Court held that a plaintiff can file a claim for breach of fiduciary duty by failing to properly monitor investments, as long as the alleged breach of the continuing duty occurred within the statutory period. The lower courts erred by applying the statutory framework based solely on the initial choice of funds, so the Court remanded to the Ninth Circuit for reconsideration.

It would be easy to assume that this decision applied solely to ERISA plan managers and their advisors or that it required automatic review of certain share classes held as plan assets. However, the *Tibble* decision should be seen in a broader context: all trustees have an ongoing duty to monitor the appropriateness of their investments even after they are selected initially. This duty applies not only to the selection of classes of shares or funds but also more broadly to the choice of one fund or another. This is particularly true in the case of index

5. Tibble v. Edison Int'l, 575 U.S. 523 (2015).
6. *Id.* at 529.

funds (for example, a fund that tracks the S&P 500): the trustee must take ongoing care that such funds have (all things being equal) the lowest cost among their competitors. The individual trustee who has delegated her responsibility of investing trust assets to an advisor must periodically ensure that that advisor is monitoring such expenses.

9

Investment Directions in the Trust Instrument

Given the default duty of trustees to diversify investments, regardless of the assets originally contributed to the trustee, the next question is whether and to what extent a grantor can override that duty in the trust agreement. While the answer, in the abstract at least, is that a grantor can override that obligation, the language needed to do so, and the scope of possible exculpation, is not as broad as most clients might think. This is another aspect of a trustee's investment duties that has generated a great deal of litigation.

A. Restatement Standard

The first drafting issue likely to arise is the definition of the trustee's "discretion." According to the Restatement, if a trust agreement provides that investments may be made "in the trustee's discretion" or confers on the trustee "all of the powers of an owner," such language will not ordinarily be construed as granting broader discretion than that conferred by the UPIA. Therefore, the standard of review will be the same as if that language had been left out. Trust agreements that grant the trustee "absolute" or "sole and uncontrolled" discretion in investment matters broaden the trustee's "latitude in investment matters," but such latitude is not unlimited. However, this "extended investment discretion" ordinarily is interpreted "as lessening the degree of caution or conservatism ordinarily required of the trustee . . . and as permitting in general a greater than normal latitude in the development of an investment strategy."[1] It also may allow the trustee "greater latitude in judgments concerning the 'income' and 'productivity' of investments."[2]

The comments to section 228 point out that directions and restrictions in the trust agreement regarding investments are "legally permissible and are

1. Restatement (Third) of Trusts § 91 [1992 § 228], at 109 (Am. L. Inst. 1992).
2. *Id.*

ordinarily binding on the trustee in managing the trust assets, thus often displacing the normal duty of prudence." However, the trustee may not be under a duty to "comply with a term of the trust if a court order directs or authorizes non-compliance when, as a result of circumstances not known or anticipated by the settlor, compliance would defeat or substantially impair the accomplishment of the purposes of the trust." In that case, "the trustee may have a duty to apply to the court for permission to deviate" from the trust terms.[3]

Further, if a trust agreement merely "authorizes" a particular investment, it is permissive only; the trustee is not under a duty to retain investments permitted under such a provision. It is unclear "the degree to which the trustee may have to give special consideration to specifically authorized investments, as against simply omitting them from serious consideration." What is clear, however, is that a permissive provision does not "remove the trustee of the fundamental duty to act with prudence."[4] Further, mere investment authorization does not "constitute an exculpatory clause." Because these permissive provisions do not relieve the trustee of the duty to act prudently, and because diversification is a fundamental part of trustee investment requirements, "trust provisions are strictly construed against dispensing with that requirement altogether."[5]

Put another way, any trust provision that simply authorizes, rather than explicitly directs, a trustee to hold a high concentration of a single asset or type of investment should not be relied on by a trustee without taking further steps.

B. Prudent Investor Act Standard

By contrast, the UPIA says very little about the ability to override the duty to diversify or the ability to exculpate a trustee for failing to do so. As already noted, section 1 of the Prudent Investor Act states that it is a "default rule," which may be expanded, restricted or eliminated by the trust terms. If the Prudent Investor Act is not overridden, the trustee owes a duty to the beneficiaries of the trust to comply with the Prudent Investor Rule. This seemingly broad statement might lead a lawyer to believe that she has wide latitude in overriding the duty to diversify and exculpating trustees. However, in light of the provisions of the Restatement just described, and the case law (described next), such is probably not the case.

C. Case Law

This section, dealing with the ability of a grantor to override the duty to diversify in the trust agreement, and the ability to exculpate the trustee from liability

3. *Id.* § 91 [1992 § 228], at 104–05 (comment).
4. *Id.* at 106.
5. *Id.* at 106–07.

for failing to diversify, is probably the most important and controversial in the entire book. Several decisions in recent years have produced counterintuitive (and troublesome) results.

In a Minnesota case,[6] the decedent's testamentary trust was funded 98 percent with stock in the decedent's closely held business. This business was later acquired by Borden, Inc., and, as of 1980, 98 percent of the trust assets consisted of Borden stock. The trustees were a corporate trustee and two individuals (brothers), one of whom was the plaintiff. Although the trustees did sell a significant amount of stock, Borden stock still made up 40 percent of the trust assets after the sale. The plaintiff trustee voted to continue to diversify, but the other two trustees voted to hold the stock until it recovered some of its lost value. The stock ultimately dropped from $36 per share to $14 per share. When the plaintiff sought to surcharge the corporate trustee for the losses, the trustee asserted that the trust's exculpation clause protected it from liability. The clause stated that

> [n]o Trustee shall be liable for the fault or doing of any other Trustee, whether the act be one of misfeasance or nonfeasance, nor shall he be held liable for any loss by reason of any mistake or errors in judgment made by him in good faith in the execution of the trust.[7]

The trial court dismissed the action on the basis of this clause; however, the appellate court remanded, holding that, although the exculpation clause was not void as against public policy, it would not protect the corporate trustee if the losses were due to negligence. Exculpation clauses are to be strictly construed against the trustee; here, the clause protected only against "mere errors in judgment," not negligence. Following remand, the trial court found that the losses were due to negligence, and Norwest Bank again appealed, this time on the trial court's finding of surcharges of more than $4 million. In a second decision, the appellate court again upheld the lower court.[8]

Interestingly, one of the most significant cases in this area is an unreported trial court decision that was overturned.[9] In this case, a testator will created a trust for the benefit first of his wife, then of his daughter, and finally of her issue. The testator died in 1956. His testamentary trust contained the following language:

> It is my desire and hope that said stock will be held by my said Executors and my said Trustee to be distributed to the ultimate beneficiaries under this Will, and neither my Executors nor my said Trustee shall dispose of such stock for the purpose of diversification of investment and neither they or it shall be held

6. *In re* Trusteeship of Williams, 591 N.W.2d 743 (Minn. Ct. App. 1999), *aff'd*, 631 N.W.2d 398 (Minn. Ct. App. 2001).

7. *Id.* at 746.

8. *In re* Williams, 631 N.W.2d 398 (Minn. Ct. App. 2001).

9. *In re* Chase Manhattan Bank, 809 N.Y.S.2d 360 (App. Div. 2006), *rev'g* 791 N.Y.S.2d 868 (Sur. Ct. 2004).

> liable for any diminution in the value of such stock. * * * * The foregoing provisions shall not prevent my said Executors or my said Trustee from disposing of all or part of the stock of Eastman Kodak Company in case there shall be some compelling reason other than diversification of investment for doing so.[10]

A corporate fiduciary was named trustee. Ninety-five percent of the trust assets consisted of shares in Eastman Kodak Company. In 1972, the testator's wife died. The trustee filed its first intermediate accounting, showing that the stock was still the main trust asset, to which no objections were made. Despite a significant decline in the value of Kodak stock, the trustee held the stock for approximately 34 years. In 1997, attorneys for a beneficiary approached the trustee about selling the Kodak stock, but the trustee did nothing. The beneficiary filed a compulsory accounting, the bank filed a petition for settlement of its second account in 1998, and the beneficiary objected. She sought damages in excess of $39,000,000 resulting from the improper retention of Kodak stock.

The Surrogate (writing the decision) pointed out that a clause authorizing retention of a single holding "cannot trump the application of prudence in the management of an estate." Under New York law, if a retention clause conflicts with the legal duty of prudence imposed upon a fiduciary, "the clause must lose." The trustee had full authority to sell the Kodak stock, and "the language which authorized the sale of stock is worded much more strongly than the language which urges retention." The retention language was "clearly precatory." According to the Surrogate, the most important sentence of the entire will was the one allowing disposition of all or part of the Kodak stock "in case there shall be some compelling reason other than diversification of investment for doing so." The Surrogate interpreted this clause to mean that the trustee was not to sell simply in order to diversify even if the Kodak stock was performing well; rather, the trustee was to sell the stock if there were some other compelling reason, such as poor performance. In other words, selling for the purpose of diversification itself was "preemptive" and was not required; it was not the same as selling to "remedy a suffered loss." The trustee never defined for itself the meaning of the term "compelling reason" until the beneficiary approached it about sale. Further, it was troubling that the trustee "adhered to the proposed proposition that the Kodak retention itself was the purpose of the trust" and not the care of the testator's family. In fact, the Surrogate held that under New York law, the "complete lack of documentation alone is itself a breach of trust." As a result of all of these findings (as well as several others), the Surrogate found the trustee liable, and it was surcharged almost $21,000,000.[11]

---

10. *In re Chase*, 809 N.Y.S.2d at 362.

11. *In re* Judicial Settlement of the Second Intermediate Account of Chase Manhattan Bank, 791 N.Y.S.2d 868 (Sur. Ct. 2004), *rev'd*, 809 N.Y.S.2d 360 (App. Div. 2006).

The Supreme Court of New York, however, overturned the Surrogate's ruling.[12] First, the Surrogate determined, on its own motion, the date on which damages began; the decision that the trustee should have sold on that date was made solely in hindsight. The court also found that the low income yield of the stock, which the Surrogate found significant in holding that the trustee should have sold the stock in 1974, actually was not a compelling reason to sell. The dispositive test was not the income yield in the abstract but whether it was reasonable for the needs of the particular beneficiary. Given the beneficiary's other wealth, the income yield was adequate for her circumstances, even though it may have been low in the abstract. At least one commentator has observed that, while the appellate court's decision may provide comfort to the particular trustee in this decision, it provides little comfort to other trustees holding large single-stock positions, because the appellate decision focuses narrowly on two procedural issues.[13]

The problem with the Surrogate's decision in *Dumont* that the appellate court did not address was the way in which it questions any language that purports to allow assets to be retained without diversifying or the grantor to exculpate the trustee for retaining such holdings. The lawyer drafting Mr. Dumont's will probably thought that the stock retention provision gave the trustee complete discretion to hold the stock regardless of any change in circumstance. The *Dumont* decision, however, says otherwise.

In a New York decision,[14] a corporate trustee of a trust that was funded in 1966 with a block of the trustee's own stock and stock in 18 other corporations liquidated all that stock (including its own) and invested the proceeds in its common trust funds. A beneficiary sued, arguing that the trust agreement allowed the trustee to retain its own common stock and also that it achieved lower investment results than a "prudent investor" would have. Treating the trustee's investment in its own common trust funds as diversification, the court found that the trustee correctly sold its own stock, regardless of the ability given to hold the stock in the instrument, because "[n]either the trust language permitting retention of the stock nor the preferences of the trust beneficiaries would have insulated [the trustee] from a claim that it breached its fiduciary duty had it failed to achieve appropriate diversification."[15] Thus, in this case the Prudent Investor Act served as a shield for the trustee from liability, rather than as a weapon to be used against it. This case again makes clear that trust language authorizing undiversified holdings does not really relieve the trustee from its duty to diversify.

A different result would probably have been achieved in Pennsylvania. In a Fourth Circuit affirmation of a lower court's holding,[16] the court held that a trustee authorized to retain property would not be held liable for failure to

12. *In re Chase Manhattan Bank*, 809 N.Y.S.2d 360.

13. Jonathan J. Rikoon, *Dumont Reversed*, Trs. & Ests. 56 (2006).

14. *In re* Strong, 289 A.D.2d 798 (N.Y. App. Div. 2001).

15. *Id.* at 800.

16. Stopper v. Kestel, 11 Fed. App'x 369 (4th Cir. 2001) (unpublished decision).

diversify under Pennsylvania law unless the plaintiff meets the stringent test of "supine negligence" or "willful default." The Fourth Circuit noted that the trustee was not required to diversify trust investments under Pennsylvania law and that nondiversification is not presumptively imprudent. Rather, the standard for imposing liability on a trustee authorized to retain investments is "supine negligence or willful default." No evidence was presented that the trustee acted in bad faith or with indolence, supine negligence, or willful default, nor that the stock was undervalued. Consequently, the trustee was relieved of any liability.[17] This case is probably of limited value outside of Pennsylvania, however, since the Prudent Investor Act is not even mentioned in the decision.

An Ohio case,[18] while reaching a similar conclusion to that in *Dumont*, provides at least some guidance regarding the type of language that can be used to allow a trustee to retain assets. In this case, the grantor created a trust worth over $8 million for the benefit of his wife. Eighty percent of the trust assets were in the form of the stock of the corporate trustee, Firstar Bank. The trust agreement stated that the trustee was permitted to retain, manage, and invest the stock in the trust "as they deem advisable or proper." The trust also included a retention clause that allowed the trustee to retain its own stock. Specifically, the trustee had the power "to retain any securities in the same form as when received, including shares of a corporate trustee . . . , even though all of such securities are not of the class of investments a trustee may be permitted by law to make and to hold cash un-invested as they deem advisable or proper." The court noted the "unfortunate wording"; it was unclear whether the term "advisable or proper" applied only to cash and not to other assets. Although it was unnecessary to construe this language in this case, the court warned that "this type of fuzzy drafting can create problems."[19]

The trustee held its own stock and did not diversify. In fact, it liquidated assets other than its own stock to raise funds to pay estate taxes. Within a year of the grantor's death, both the beneficiary and her financial advisor asked the trustee to sell some of its stock. Neither request was made in writing, and the trustee did not sell any stock. Shortly thereafter, the Firstar stock dropped in value by $770,000. The beneficiaries sued the trustee for failing to diversify. The trustee argued consent and ratification, because the trustee had met with the beneficiaries to discuss the trust terms.

The court held that the language allowing the trustee to retain its own stock "merely served to circumvent the rule of undivided loyalty. The trust did not say anything about diversification."[20] Citing the Restatement (Third) of Trusts, the court held that a general authorization in the terms of the trust "to retain investments received as a part of a trust estate does not ordinarily abrogate the

17. *Id.* at *6.
18. Wood v. U.S. Bank, N.A., 160 Ohio App. 3d 831 (Ct. App. 2005).
19. *Id.* at 835.
20. *Id.* at 839.

trustee's duty with respect to diversification or the trustee's general duty to act with prudence in investment matters." As a result, the court held that, "to abrogate the duty to diversify, the trust must contain specific language authorizing or directing the trustee to retain in a specific investment a larger percentage of the trust assets than would normally be prudent."[21]

An Ohio decision,[22] dealing with a charitable remainder unitrust (CRUT), addresses the extent to which trust language can direct nondiversification. Here, the grantor established a charitable remainder trust with Firstar Bank funded solely with $2 million of Procter & Gamble (P&G) stock. The trust agreement stated that the trustee's powers included the power to

> retain, without liability for loss or depreciation resulting from such retention, original property, real or personal, received from grantor or from any other source, although it may represent a disproportionate part of the trust.

According to the grantor, Firstar knew that one of the purposes of the trust was to diversify out of that concentrated holding. Firstar's investment officer started to sell the P&G stock but stopped when its price dropped. Although the diversification process resumed when the price went back up, at the end of the first year, the value of the trust assets had dropped by half.

The grantor removed Firstar Bank as trustee and appointed Fifth Third Bank as successor trustee, which then filed a claim against Firstar Bank for breach of fiduciary duty. At trial, several witnesses testified that the trust agreement did not require the trustee to diversify but also that it did not relieve the trustee from that duty and that the trustee's behavior was governed by the Ohio Prudent Investor Act, which ordinarily required diversification.[23] Firstar objected to this testimony. The court allowed the testimony because it was not offered to contradict the clear terms of the trust but rather was directed at the purpose of the trust. In fact, the court stated that Firstar itself "opened the door to much of the testimony when it suggested that the CRUT did not require it to diversify."[24]

Firstar Bank also argued that the trust exculpated it from any liability for the losses in the value of trust assets. Holding against Firstar Bank, the court cited the *Wood* case,[25] which stated that "[e]ven if the trust document allows the trustee to 'retain' assets that would not normally be suitable, the trustee's duty remains, unless there are special circumstances."[26]

The duty to diversify could be modified only if the document "clearly indicates an intention to abrogate the common-law, now statutory, duty to

---

21. *Id.* at 840.

22. Fifth Third Bank v. Firstar Bank, N.A., Appeal No. C-050518, 2006 WL 2520329 (Ohio Ct. App. Sept. 1, 2006).

23. *Id.*

24. *Id.* at 17.

25. Wood v. U.S. Bank, N.A., 160 Ohio App. 3d 831 (Ct. App. 2005).

26. *Id.* at 2.

diversify."[27] The court found that the CRUT language in this case did not clearly indicate such an intention. Further, even if the trust language relieved Firstar Bank of its duty to diversify, the investment officer failed to verify relevant investment and management facts; he did not properly take into account the economic conditions, tax consequences, and liquidity needs when he chose to sell the P&G stock gradually over the course of the year.

This case presents another example of poor administration choices resulting in bad case law. Even though the trust language, by itself, seems to relieve the trustee of liability for failure to diversify, the trustee's behavior essentially nullified the potential effect of that language. The whole point of creating a CRUT funded with a concentration of a single stock is to diversify out of that position while delaying or avoiding the capital gains consequences. Further, Firstar Bank did start to diversify but did it badly, arguing only after the fact that it had no duty to diversify.

However, an Indiana decision goes the other way. In this case,[28] National City Bank of Indiana (the Bank) created an estate plan, by court order, for an incapacitated member of the Lilly family. (The decision refers to that person as the "decedent"; however, she is at the time of this writing still alive.) At the time that the decedent became incapacitated, her estate plan according to the Bank was complex and inefficient, likely to result in both litigation and estate-tax liability. The Bank petitioned the court to establish a new estate plan, a key piece of which was the creation of two testamentary charitable remainder annuity trusts (the CRATs). The decision notes that several prestigious law firms spent hundreds of hours reviewing, commenting on, and objecting to the terms of these trusts on behalf of not only the Bank but also the charitable remainder beneficiaries. After this extensive review process, the court approved the plan.

Both CRATs granted to the trustee the power

> *[t]o retain indefinitely any property received by the trustee* and invest and reinvest the trust property in stocks, bonds, mortgages, notes, shares of stock of regulated investment companies or other property of any kind, real or personal, . . . *and any investment made or retained by the trustee in good faith shall be proper despite any resulting risk or lack of diversification or marketability and although not of a kind considered by law suitable for trust investments.*[29]

The CRATs were funded with about $286 million of stock in Eli Lilly and Company. Two to three months later, the Bank prepared a draft investment plan with respect to the CRATs. However, most of the stock was not sold until ten months after funding, during which time the value of the stock had dropped significantly. The beneficiaries objected to the Bank's petition for approval of its accountings, claiming the Bank breached its fiduciary duty by allowing the value of the stock to drop by delaying the stock sales. The Bank then claimed that the trust agreement

27. Fifth Third Bank, *supra* note 22, at 23.
28. Ams. for the Arts v. Nat'l City Bank of Ind., 855 N.E.2d 592 (2006).
29. *Id.* at 595.

eliminated its duty to comply with the Prudent Investor Act and exculpated it from any liability as a result of its failure to diversify. The beneficiaries responded that the clause was invalid because it was inserted by the Bank for its own protection.

The court began by first noting the beneficiaries' silence during the drafting process of the CRATs. Their lawyers reviewed and commented on many provisions of these trusts but never on the cited paragraph. The court seemed to sympathize with the Bank, noting that it had voluntarily stepped in to make the decedent's estate plan more straightforward and tax-efficient and gave all the beneficiaries ample time to review and comment on the documents. The court ruled that, because the beneficiaries "chose not to quarrel with any portion of paragraph 10(b), . . . they are not now entitled to turn back the clock and claim that, in hindsight, the clauses are problematic and unenforceable."[30] Further, in light of the amount of review of the plan that took place, the Bank was not obligated to call the cited paragraph to any party's attention. The court also held that the Bank was not self-dealing when it included that paragraph, in part because the Bank received no benefit or profit at the expense of the beneficiaries and because the probate court approved the CRAT terms prior to their enactment.

Turning to the actual trust language, and noting this was a case of first impression, the court held that, because the clause explicitly lessened the duty to diversify, as allowed under a recent Ohio case,[31] the cited paragraph was sufficient to override the general duty to diversify. Finally, the court found the exculpatory clause was valid, rejecting the beneficiaries' claims that the Bank acted "with reckless indifference,"[32] thus nullifying the effect of that clause. Because the Bank in this case was not liable for breach, the statute cited by the beneficiaries that would have invalidated the clause could not apply.

What these cases demonstrate is that bad trustee behavior can result in published decisions that have a negative impact on all trustees. In the two charitable remainder trust cases, the trustees each failed to diversify investments in a timely manner, in contradiction of the purpose of the trusts. Yet one trustee was protected by nondiversification and exculpation language, while the other was not. Perhaps the only deciding factor is the amount of communication with the beneficiaries. In *Americans for the Arts*, the drafting process was well documented, the beneficiaries were all very well informed before the document was executed, and they were well informed during the year after execution. The same cannot be said for *Fifth Third Bank*. Trustee communication, it seems, will trump trust language, which is probably the correct result.

Finally, a Kansas decision[33] held that a letter from the grantor of a revocable trust to the corporate trustee directing it to retain certain stock will override the trustee's duty to diversify the holdings. Here, the trust agreement stated that,

30. *Id.* at 598.

31. *Wood*, 160 Ohio App. 3d 831.

32. *Ams. for the Arts*, 855 N.E.2d at 602.

33. McGinley v. Bank of Am., N.A., 279 Kan. 426 (2005).

during the grantor's lifetime, the trustee was to consult her as to any purchase or sale of trust assets and abide by her decisions unless, in the trustee's sole opinion, the grantor is incapable of managing her own affairs.[34] In this case, the grantor delivered significant amounts of Enron stock to the corporate trustee, instructed it by letter to hold the stock as trust assets, and exculpated the trustee from liability as a result of doing so. The court held that the trust language and the letter from the grantor relieved the trustee of liability. This decision turned, it seems, on the facts that the trust was revocable and that it was the grantor, and not some other beneficiary, who had written the letter. This is, of course, the correct result and is not especially controversial.

34. *Id.* at 429.

10

Determining Breach and Damages

This chapter addresses the manner in which a breach is determined and the calculation of damages in the event of such a breach.

A. Restatement and Prudent Investor Act Standards

The Restatement reinforces the fact that the determination of "whether a breach of trust has occurred turns on the prudence of the trustee's conduct, not on the eventual results of investment decisions."[1] The Restatement provides three examples of trustee behavior that may or may not lead to liability in the event of loss. Interestingly, in the two favorable illustrations, the trustee has invested in securities that, though prudent when chosen, nevertheless result in loss due to a downturn in general economic conditions. On the other hand, the example that gives rise to liability is of a trustee who invests some of the funds in carefully selected real estate investments. Despite the conscientious efforts of the trustee, the trust agreement prohibits investment in real estate, and therefore the trustee would be liable for any resulting loss from the investment due to the specific breach of the trust agreement.

Section 8 of the UPIA reinforces this point: compliance with the prudent investor rule "is determined in light of the facts and circumstances existing at the time of a trustee's decision or action and not by hindsight." As the comments point out, "[t]rustees are not insurers * * * . Not every investment or management decision will turn out in the light of hindsight to have been successful. Hindsight is not the relevant standard."

1. Restatement (Third) of Trusts 11 (Am. L. Inst. 1992).

B. Case Law

Perhaps the most important decision for determining damages came from New York's highest court.[2] Here, a decedent created testamentary trusts funded primarily with a $2,500,000 stock portfolio, 71 percent of which was made up of Eastman Kodak Company stock. The trustee sold only enough Kodak shares to pay administration expenses and retained the balance of the shares for seven years. During this time, the shares' value dropped to approximately one-third of their value at the date of the decedent's death. The beneficiaries sued for failure to diversify.

The court found three separate breaches of the duty to diversify. First, the trustee failed to consider the Kodak stock in relation to the entire investment portfolio. Second, because the annual yield from the portfolio was only 1.7 percent, the high concentration of Kodak stock "jeopardized the interests of the primary income beneficiary of the estate."[3] Third, the trustee may have failed to exercise due care "and the skill it held itself out as possessing as a corporate fiduciary."[4]

The court then turned to the measure of damages. The lower court adopted a "lost profits" measure of damages, under which the damages were calculated to be what the proceeds of the Kodak stock would have yielded, to the time of trial, "had they been invested in [the trustee's] own diversified equity fund on August 9, 1973."[5] The *Janes* court overturned this determination and instead found that the appropriate damages should be based on the value of the stock on the date it should have been sold (in this case, shortly after the decedent died), reduced by the proceeds from the actual sale of the stock. Further, the trial court in its discretion could award interest. The court found that the "lost profits" measure of damages was appropriate only where "the fiduciary's misconduct consisted of deliberate self-dealing and faithless transfers of trust property."[6]

Two New York Supreme Court cases[7] followed *Janes*. Both were decided the same day, and both involved trustees who held IBM stock as essentially the sole trust asset. In *Saxton*, the decedent created a trust funded entirely with IBM stock. In 1960, two years after the trust was created, the corporate fiduciary (the Bank) sent an "Investment Direction Agreement" to the beneficiaries, under which they agreed that they wanted the trustee to continue to hold the IBM stock as the sole trust asset, rather than to diversify. The trustee did not discuss with the beneficiaries the agreement or the risks associated with not diversifying.

2. Matter of the Estate of Janes, 90 N.Y.2d 41 (1997).
3. *Id.* at 53–54.
4. *Id.*
5. *Id.* at 48.
6. *Id.* at 55.
7. Estate of Saxton, 712 N.Y.S.2d 225 (2000); Matter of Rowe, 274 A.D.2d 87 (N.Y. App. Div. 2000).

For the next 19 years, the trustee did not communicate with the beneficiaries. Twenty-four years after the trust was created, the beneficiaries began to ask the trustee to diversify the trust investments. However, the trustee did not prepare or present any plans to do so. The trust officer's position was that holding one security alone was adequate so long as that security remained on the Bank's "buy" list, even though the Bank's own written investment policies recognized that diversification was required under the "prudent person rule."[8] In 1992, the trustee finally implemented a diversification strategy, at which point the value of the stock had dropped by more than $4 million. At this point, of course, the beneficiaries sued the trustee for breach of fiduciary duty.

The trustee alleged that the agreement protected it from liability and that the beneficiaries consented to the stock retention. The court, however, held that the trustee breached its duty in 1987, when the beneficiaries informed the trustee that it was obligated to develop a diversification strategy. The court applied equitable, rather than contractual, standards in finding that the agreement did not protect the trustee and adopted the *Janes* method for determining damages.

The *Rowe* case dealt with a charitable lead trust initially funded solely with IBM stock. As in *Saxton*, the corporate trustee had a written diversification policy, under which a single security should not constitute more than 10 percent of the total assets of a trust. Nevertheless, the trustee decided not to diversify because the IBM stock had dropped in value from the date of trust funding. Instead, the trustee decided to diversify "at a later time when the stock had reached a higher price."[9] The trustee began to diversify two years after funding, but three years after that, the trust still held approximately two-thirds of its original IBM stake, at which point the value of the stock had dropped from $3.5 million to $1.8 million. The trustee was sued for breach of fiduciary duty. The beneficiaries' expert witness stated that the trustee's "tactic of waiting for the IBM stock to rise was based on 'wishful hoping' . . . ."[10] The court found the trustee liable and used the *Janes* method of determining damages. Finally, the *Janes* method of calculating damages was also confirmed by a federal district court, which specifically rejected the S&P 500 measure of damages.[11]

Not all state courts have followed *Janes*, however. A Maine court, for example, was open to the idea of a lost profits measure of damages.[12] In this case, the surviving spouse and trustee "retained some of the assets, sold others, and commingled both the assets and the proceeds with his own personal assets."[13] Following the trustee's death, the personal representative of his estate filed an accounting stating that the estate was liable to the successor trustee for the value

8. *Saxton*, 712 N.Y.S.2d at 228.
9. *Rowe*, 274 A.D.2d at 90.
10. *Id.* at 92.
11. Williams v. J.P. Morgan & Co., 248 F. Supp. 2d 320 (S.D.N.Y. 2003).
12. Estate of Wilde, 708 A.2d 273 (1998).
13. *Id.*

of the assets the surviving spouse did not transfer to the trust at the date of death. The successor trustee, on the other hand, asserted that "the damages should be determined not with reference to the increase in value of the inception assets but by reference to the value that would have been attained" in an S&P 500 index fund.[14]

The court observed that the parties agreed that the damages caused by the husband's breach should be determined by reference to the performance of a prudent professional trustee in Portland, Maine, managing family trusts similar to the decedent's trust.[15] By implication, the parties also agreed that a prudent trustee would not have invested all of the assets in an S&P 500 index fund. As a result, the court was required to follow the measure of damages agreed to by the parties and could not impose its own S&P 500 index fund measure of damages (as the trial court had done). However, the court noted that "[h]ad the [trial court] had reliable facts before it from which it could have found that a prudent trustee would have used either the more aggressive or the more conservative investment strategy, it could have determined damages with reference to such strategies."[16] In other words, using an index fund's return as the measure of return that should have been obtained was inappropriate, but only because the parties already had stipulated as to the appropriate measure of damages.

14. *Id.*
15. *Id.*
16. *Id.*

11

Extending the Reach of the Prudent Investor Act

As with all aspects of the law, a statute is only as good as the case law interpreting it. Because the Prudent Investor Act is a little over ten years old, the case law referring to it is only now starting to emerge. Further, much of the case law is "unreported," which means that, while you can find it through internet research, it is not entered into the official reporting services and therefore in most states cannot be cited as precedent. (In other words, it's not gossip, but in some situations, not a lot better.)

A. Does the Prudent Investor Act Govern Relationships with Individuals?

The Prudent Investor Act states explicitly that it applies to trustees. So why even ask the question? Because in at least one case, that's exactly what the plaintiff did. In an unreported Washington decision,[1] a plaintiff had an investment management account with a corporate investment advisor. In 1996, during the big equity ride, the plaintiff signed off on an investment policy, reflecting her investment goals, that targeted an investment allocation of 65 to 85 percent equity investments. Throughout their relationship, the investment advisor confirmed that the plaintiff had a high level of risk tolerance. The advisor provided a great deal of written information about market history and volatility, and there was a significant amount of communication with the plaintiff generally. Nevertheless, when the stock market took its inevitable turn for the worse, and after the plaintiff continued to make significant monthly withdrawals from the account, she sued the advisor for damages, alleging that the advisor had breached its investment agreement, its fiduciary duty, and the Washington version of the Prudent Investor Act. With respect to the last allegation, the plaintiff argued that an investment account

1. Hatheway v. U.S. Trust Co., N.A., 136 Wash. App. 1044, 2007 WL 120841 (2007).

manager owes a greater fiduciary duty than a general fiduciary does, and therefore the advisor should be held to the Prudent Investor Act standard.

The court, finding for the advisor, ruled in part that the advisor was simply an agent, not a trustee, and therefore the Prudent Investor Act standards could not be applied to it. The advisor owed the plaintiff the duties of loyalty, care, and full disclosure, and the trustee discharged those duties. In particular, the advisor was loyal to the plaintiff's stated investment goals. In finding for the advisor, the court also awarded the advisor its attorney fees.

This was, of course, the correct result. What is disturbing, however, is the fact that the advisor had to take the case to the appellate level before obtaining that result. While it is true that anyone can file a lawsuit, it might be worth making clear, when providing investment advice to individuals, what the proper level of oversight should be (not necessarily in the investment policy statement, but perhaps in correspondence). Further, ongoing communication with a client is critical to ensuring that an errant court doesn't apply a more stringent standard simply because there was a lack of communication.

B. Applying the Prudent Investor Act to Estates as Well as Trusts

Trustees are not the only fiduciaries to whom the UPIA may apply. Several states impose those standards on executors or administrators of estates.[2] Two New York decisions deal with the application of the Prudent Investor Act in this context. In the first,[3] the decedent employed her longtime attorney, following his retirement from the practice of law, as her investment advisor for $17,000 per month. When the decedent's death was imminent, he advanced himself $85,000 in fees as financial advisor. Upon the decedent's death, the attorney was named as coexecutor, along with the attorney's longtime assistant (who, apparently, performed only ministerial duties and exercised no independent discretion). During the administration process, and nearly three years after the decedent's death, the attorney moved at least half the remaining assets from New York to Florida (where the attorney lived) without seeking either beneficiary or court approval. He then authorized, or at least ratified, an inappropriate investment of estate assets in a junk bond mutual fund. For the next 17 months, the attorney ignored the investment, resulting in significant losses. When the executors filed their accounting, the sole estate beneficiary objected on numerous grounds and the Surrogate's Court imposed surcharges on the executors, denied commissions to the attorney, and removed him as a fiduciary, finding that he intentionally and unreasonably delayed making distributions to the beneficiary, motivated out

2. *See, e.g.*, N.Y. Est. Powers & Trusts Law § 11-2.3 2022.
3. *In re* Estate of Witherill, 37 A.D.3d 879 (N.Y. App. Div. 2007).

of spite (because the beneficiary was suing him over a charitable remainder unitrust he had set up for the decedent, naming the attorney and his wife as income beneficiaries). The appellate court upheld the Surrogate's conclusions.

This case doesn't teach much, because it was clearly the product of apparently malicious (or at least incompetent) behavior by the attorney. However, there are a couple of notable points. First, the appellate court found that his "gross departure" from his obligations constituted "faithless misfeasance" and therefore justified the imposition of "lost profit or lost appreciation damages," which is a more severe measure of damages that is the norm in New York.[4] Second, the court held that "the fact that other investments might have appreciated in value or fared less well [did] not insulate" the attorney from liability.[5]

The next case,[6] which is unpublished, also addresses a contested accounting by a New York executor. Here, the decedent held dual U.S./Taiwan citizenship. He had three children by a prior marriage as well as two from his marriage to the executor. (Guess who objected to the accounting.) The decedent had a net worth of approximately $6.7 million, which included stocks and real property in Taiwan. The children from the first marriage filed 19 objections to the accounting. Among them was the fact that the executor had taken six months to obtain letters of administration. The court denied the executor's motion for summary judgment, noting that this was an issue of fact and that under New York law she had a duty to prevent losses by taking prompt measures to preserve estate assets. The other objection that is important for purposes of this discussion is the children's allegation that there was a delay in selling a block of 1,500 shares of IBM stock, which resulted in a loss. The stock was liquidated to correspond to the payment of state and federal estate taxes. The net losses amounted to about $9,800. The court, granting the executor summary judgment on this issue, stated that "[t]he prudent investor rule is a rule of conduct, not outcome or performance," and that in this case, selling stock as taxes become due resulting in relatively small losses in a large estate is not imprudent. Interestingly, the court contradicted itself by looking at the outcome (which was relatively small in a large estate) even though it stated it was not to do so.

These cases demonstrate a few fairly obvious principles. As a preliminary matter, even though many if not most states do not impose the Prudent Investor Act standards on estate executors (since they apply only to express trusts), it is probably a good idea for an executor to assume that those standards will be applied to estate investment standards. If that is the case, then an executor must consider the investment time horizon (which, with most estates, will be short) and whether original assets are to be retained. This is a different analysis than with trusts, for obvious reasons: an executor cannot "diversify out" of assets that are specifically

4. *See Estate of Saxton* and *Matter of Rowe*, discussed *infra* ch. 10.

5. Witherill, *supra* note 3, at 881.

6. *In re* Su-Lien Chen, 16 Misc. 3d 1107(A), 2007 WL 1965810 (N.Y. Sur. 2007).

devised, for example. However, creating a written investment strategy for estate assets is probably a worthwhile exercise for executors, and (as with trusts) communicating that strategy to beneficiaries as soon as possible is critical. Indeed, given that most assets will have a stepped-up basis for income tax purposes, selling assets to come up with a short-term strategy has added importance (unless of course the assets have a special relationship to the grantor or the family).

Following up on this idea of short time horizons, in a pair of cases from North Carolina,[7] a corporate trustee (not an executor) was holding disputed funds pending a determination of whether those funds were to be characterized as income or principal. These disputed funds were invested at a very low rate, yielding between 0.720 percent and 1.58 percent. The corporate fiduciary also was holding assets that were treated as principal that yielded between 4.565 percent and 5.208 percent. The income beneficiary filed a claim against the corporate fiduciary, alleging that the disputed funds should have been invested in the same tax-exempt municipal bond fund in which principal was held. The corporate fiduciary filed for summary judgment and the court granted it. The court first noted that the corporate fiduciary had obligations to both the income and remainder beneficiaries and also noted the long history of litigation between the income beneficiary (who was the second wife) and the remainder beneficiaries (who, of course, were children from the prior marriage). The court next observed that the corporate fiduciary was "well within its discretion to consider a potential settlement and a resulting need for liquidity in its decision to keep the Retained Funds in a money market account. The relevant statute explicitly authorizes trustees to consider '[n]eeds for liquidity' in managing trust assets."[8] Further, law of another jurisdiction indicated that "it is proper for trustees faced with conflicting claims to funds to keep the funds as liquid as possible."[9] Because settlement could have come at any time, the corporate trustee was justified in keeping the assets as liquid as possible. In this regard, there was no issue of material fact and the court ruled in favor of the corporate fiduciary. In the second case, decided on the same day, the court also found that it was proper for the corporate fiduciary to pay its attorneys' fees from trust assets.

These cases demonstrate, although they do not say so explicitly, that a very low-yield, liquid position is appropriate where the investment horizon is very short. Although these are trust cases, an analogy can be drawn to estate cases as well. However, as with all prudent investor decisions, the best course is always to inform the beneficiaries of the investment horizon chosen and either obtain the beneficiaries' consent or at least provide the proper form for them to raise any objections.

---

7. Heinitsh v. Wachovia Bank, N.A., 2007 WL 2570300 (N.C. Super. July 14, 2007); Heinitsh v. Wachovia Bank, N.A., No. 04 CVS 734,2007 WL 2570750 (N.C. Super. June 11, 2007).

8. *Id.* at 11.

9. *Id.*

12

Effects of Principal and Income Acts on Investing

Many beneficiaries' interests are defined in terms of "income." This obviously has an effect on a trustee's investment choices because different investments generate different levels of income, and those that tend to produce more income often generate less capital appreciation than those that generate less income. This decision of whether or not to emphasize income-generating investments can often lead to a potential breach of a trustee's duty of impartiality, because the choice of income-generating investments can benefit the current beneficiary to the detriment of the remainder beneficiary.

This leads to the question of how "income" is defined. As used in trust agreements, the term "income" is defined in the income and principal act of the state in which the trust is administered. In recognition of the impact such acts can have on the interests of beneficiaries, several states have modified their principal and income acts to provide more flexibility.

In 2018, the National Conference of Commissioners on Uniform State Laws approved the Uniform Fiduciary Income and Principal Act (UFIPA). As stated in the Prefatory Note, UFIPA

> is an update of the Revised Uniform Principal and Income Act (1997). Like the 1997 Act, it adapts to changes in the design and use of trusts. Highlights include an expansion of the use of the power to adjust between income and principal in Section 203, the addition of provisions for unitrusts in Article 3, and a simplifying change in governing law for purposes of distinguishing income and principal in Section 104.[1]

1. Uniform Fiduciary Income and Principal Act, prefatory n. at 1, Unif. L. Comm'n (2018), https://www.uniformlaws.org/HigherLogic/System/DownloadDocumentFile.ashx?DocumentFileKey=0f589496-fd89-29b5-7306-f9d0292e58d9&forceDialog=0.

The comment to section 101 of UFIPA, addressing the new name, states that

> [t]he change in the name of this Uniform Act has three purposes and effects.
>
> First, this name will distinguish the 2018 Act from its 1931, 1962, and 1997 predecessors and support an acronym that will not be confused with the Uniform Prudent Investor Act, which was closely associated with the 1997 Revised Uniform Principal and Income Act.
>
> Second, by using the word "Fiduciary," the name emphasizes that the distinctions between income and principal are most likely to be relevant in the context of trusts and decedents' estates, especially trusts that continue for a long time, perpetually in the case of some modern trusts. Such trusts present a greater possibility of competing interests between those entitled to income currently and those who may be entitled to income and/or principal—that is, entitled to "what's left"—after the current interests terminate by death or otherwise. The act also applies to term relationships other than just trusts and decedents' estates, such as legal life estates, which may share the long-term character and need for balancing of successive interests that is most commonly associated with trusts. But the primary applications of the act will generally be in contexts marked by the role of a fiduciary.
>
> Third, placing income first in the name emphasizes the fact that principal may be "what's left" after income is paid out. After income is paid out it is gone and normally cannot be retrieved (although prior over-distributions can sometimes be taken into account in determining the amount of future distributions). This continues the practice of previous acts of favoring principal where there is uncertainty.[2]

While UFIPA hasn't been enacted by many states yet, it is gaining momentum, and it raises some themes that are common among many states' principal and income acts. This review will analyze only some high points of UFIPA and will not look at other previous acts (except to make note of some of the differences). Further, it will not be a comprehensive analysis of UFIPA but instead will focus on those provisions that impact investing most directly, particularly a fiduciary's ability to allocate between principal and income and to convert to and from a unitrust.

A. General Standards of Care

Before discussing the discretionary tools available to a fiduciary under UFIPA, it is helpful to review the standards applicable to those tools. Section 201(a) of UFIPA provides that,

> [i]n making an allocation or determination or exercising discretion under this [act], a fiduciary shall:
>
> (1) act in good faith, based on what is fair and reasonable to all beneficiaries;

2. *Id.* § 101 cmt.

(2) administer a trust or estate impartially, except to the extent the terms of the trust manifest an intent that the fiduciary shall or may favor one or more beneficiaries;

(3) administer the trust or estate in accordance with the terms of the trust, even if there is a different provision in this [act]; and

(4) administer the trust or estate in accordance with this [act], except to the extent the terms of the trust provide otherwise or authorize the fiduciary to determine otherwise.[3]

Section 201(b) states that a

fiduciary's allocation, determination, or exercise of discretion under this [act] is presumed to be fair and reasonable to all beneficiaries. A fiduciary may exercise a discretionary power of administration given to the fiduciary by the terms of the trust, and an exercise of the power which produces a result different from a result required or permitted by this [act] does not create an inference that the fiduciary abused the fiduciary's discretion.[4]

Under sections 201(d) and (e), a fiduciary

may exercise the power to adjust under Section 203, convert an income trust to a unitrust under Section 303(a)(1), change the percentage or method used to calculate a unitrust amount under Section 303(a)(2), or convert a unitrust to an income trust under Section 303(a)(3), if the fiduciary determines the exercise of the power will assist the fiduciary to administer the trust or estate impartially.[5]

A fiduciary must consider, when making those decisions,

(1) the terms of the trust;

(2) the nature, distribution standards, and expected duration of the trust;

(3) the effect of the allocation rules, including specific adjustments between income and principal, under [Articles] 4 through 7;

(4) the desirability of liquidity and regularity of income;

(5) the desirability of the preservation and appreciation of principal;

(6) the extent to which an asset is used or may be used by a beneficiary;

(7) the increase or decrease in the value of principal assets, reasonably determined by the fiduciary;

(8) whether and to what extent the terms of the trust give the fiduciary power to accumulate income or invade principal or prohibit the fiduciary from accumulating income or invading principal;

3. *Id.* § 201(a) at 15.
4. *Id.* § 201(b) at 15.
5. *Id.* § 201(d) at 15–16.

(9) the extent to which the fiduciary has accumulated income or invaded principal in preceding accounting periods;

(10) the effect of current and reasonably expected economic conditions; and

(11) the reasonably expected tax consequences of the exercise of the power.[6]

The comment to section 201 provides that the standard of what is fair and reasonable to all beneficiaries is "derived from Section 103(b) of the 1997 Act; it is an objective standard, not dependent on what seems to any beneficiary to be fair and reasonable."[7] The addition of the "in good faith" standard is designed to complement and support the exoneration for a fiduciary's action or inaction in good faith when deciding whether to adjust between income and principal and whether to convert to or from a unitrust or change a unitrust.

One very important change that UFIPA makes over the 1997 Act is deleting the trust "purpose" and "the intent of the settlor" as factors to consider when exercising (or not exercising) these discretionary powers. The comment states that "[d]ivining or guessing subjective elements like 'purpose' and 'intent' are not a reasonable burden to place on a fiduciary, whereas 'terms of the trust' is defined in Section 102(22)(A) to be 'the *manifestation* of the settlor's intent' in an objective medium."[8]

B. Power to Adjust

By way of background, the comment to UFIPA section 203 explains that

> [t]he power to adjust between income and principal was added to the 1997 Act . . . to complement the Uniform Prudent Investor Act . . . . The purpose of the power to adjust between income and principal was to enable a fiduciary to select investments using the standards of a prudent investor without having to realize a particular portion of the portfolio's total return in the form of traditional trust accounting income such as interest, dividends, and rents.[9]

In other words, with the mandate to invest for total return under the UPIA, trustees were finding themselves with a dilemma: the more they invested in fixed income, the greater the return to the current income beneficiaries, but the lesser the growth of principal that eventually would pass to the remainder beneficiaries. The reverse, of course, was also true with stocks. The solution provided by the 1997 Act was to allow the trustee to invest for total return but then allocate some of the principal to "income" if the return received by the income beneficiary was insufficient.

---

6. *Id.* § 201(e) at 16.
7. *Id.* § 201 cmt. at 17.
8. *Id.* at 18.
9. *Id.* § 203 cmt. at 24–25.

Section 203(a) of UFIPA provides that, except as otherwise provided in the trust terms or the section itself, "a fiduciary, in a record, without court approval, may adjust between income and principal if the fiduciary determines the exercise of the power to adjust will assist the fiduciary to administer the trust or estate impartially."[10] Subsections (b) and (c) of that section provide some protection for fiduciaries when considering whether to exercise this power: section 203 "does not create a duty to exercise or consider the power to adjust under subsection (a) or to inform a beneficiary about the applicability of this section."[11] Further, a fiduciary "that in good faith exercises or fails to exercise the power to adjust under subsection (a) is not liable to a person affected by the exercise or failure to exercise."[12]

Under section 203(d), a fiduciary should consider all relevant factors when deciding whether and to what extent to exercise the power to adjust, including those listed in section 201(e) (described earlier) and the application of sections 401(i), 408, and 413.

Section 203(e) provides a laundry list of reasons that prevent a fiduciary from exercising the power to adjust; a fiduciary may not do so if

> (1) the adjustment or determination would reduce the amount payable to a current income beneficiary from a trust that qualifies for a special tax benefit, except to the extent the adjustment is made to provide for a reasonable apportionment of the total return of the trust between the current income beneficiary and successor beneficiaries;
>
> (2) the adjustment or determination would change the amount payable to a beneficiary, as a fixed annuity or a fixed fraction of the value of the trust assets, under the terms of the trust;
>
> (3) the adjustment or determination would reduce an amount that is permanently set aside for a charitable purpose under the terms of the trust, unless both income and principal are set aside for the charitable purpose;
>
> (4) possessing or exercising the power would cause a person to be treated as the owner of all or part of the trust for federal income tax purposes;
>
> (5) possessing or exercising the power would cause all or part of the value of the trust assets to be included in the gross estate of an individual for federal estate tax purposes;
>
> (6) possessing or exercising the power would cause an individual to be treated as making a gift for federal gift tax purposes;
>
> (7) the fiduciary is not an independent person;

10. *Id.* § 203(a) at 21.
11. *Id.* § 203(b) at 21.
12. *Id.* § 203(c) at 21.

> (8) the trust is irrevocable and provides for income to be paid to the settlor and possessing or exercising the power would cause the adjusted principal or income to be considered an available resource or available income under a public-benefit program; or
>
> (9) the trust is a unitrust under [Article] 3.[13]

If the prohibitions under subsections (4), (5), (6), or (7) apply to a fiduciary, then a cofiduciary to whom those subsections do not apply may exercise the power to adjust. If there is no such cofiduciary, the fiduciary may appoint a cofiduciary (which may be a special fiduciary with limited powers) to exercise the power. Finally, a fiduciary may release or delegate to a cofiduciary the power to adjust if the fiduciary determines that its possession or exercise of the power will or may result in adverse tax consequences. However, such a release or delegation must be in a record; must apply to the entire power, unless the release or delegation provides a specific type of limitation; and must be permanent or for a limited period.[14]

Sections 203(i), (j), and (k) provide further details about the scope and nature of the exercise. First, trust terms that deny or limit the power to adjust do not affect the application of this section unless they expressly deny or limit the power to adjust under subsection (a). Second, the exercise of the power in any accounting period may apply to the current period, the immediately preceding period, and one or more subsequent periods. Third, a description of the exercise of the power to adjust under subsection (a) must be included in a report, if any, sent to beneficiaries under Uniform Trust Code section 813(c) or communicated at least annually to certain beneficiaries (including qualified beneficiaries as defined in the Uniform Trust Code if the enacting state also has enacted that uniform law).

This new section 203 provides several differences from its predecessor. The comment to section 203 provides that section 104 of the 1997 Act authorized a fiduciary to make adjustments between income and principal

> if three conditions were met: (1) the fiduciary must be managing the trust assets under the prudent investor rule; (2) the terms of the trust must express the income beneficiary's distribution rights in terms of the right to receive "income" in the sense of traditional trust accounting income; and (3) the fiduciary must be unable to comply with the duty to administer the trust impartially, based on what is fair and reasonable to all the beneficiaries, without making an adjustment. In deciding whether and to what extent to exercise the power to adjust, the fiduciary was required to consider the factors described in what is now, with refinements, Section 201(e), but the fiduciary could not make an adjustment in circumstances described in what is now, with refinements, Section 203(e).[15]

13. *Id.* § 203(e) at 21–22.
14. *Id.* § 203(h).
15. *Id.* § 203 cmt. at 25.

New section 203 eliminates the three aforementioned preconditions. The comment to that section provides that, for the power to adjust to be available, trust distributions need not be constricted by the concept of "income" in a way that economic results from year to year could arbitrarily affect.

> In other words, while the trustee of a more modern trust with greater, if not total, flexibility to make distributions from income and/or principal would actually have been denied the flexibility intended by former Section 104, new Section 203 ensures that designing a trust for greater flexibility will not ironically sacrifice the flexibility of adjustments.[16]

Section 203 does not

> empower a fiduciary to increase or decrease the degree of beneficial enjoyment to which a beneficiary is entitled under the terms of the trust; rather, it authorizes the fiduciary to make adjustments between income and principal that may be necessary or helpful if the income component of a portfolio's total return is too small or too large because of investment decisions made by the fiduciary under the prudent investor rule.[17]

New section 203(a) provides a more relaxed standard when "the fiduciary determines the exercise of the power to adjust will assist the fiduciary to administer the trust or estate impartially."[18]

As that comment further points out, section 104 of the 1997 Act "did not state the trust accounting periods to which a fiduciary's exercise of the power to adjust between income and principal would apply, suggesting that the power would be exercised year-by-year, although presumably a retrospective exercise in the first part of the following year would work."[19] Instead, UFIPA section 203(j)

> explicitly provides that an exercise of the power in 2019, for example, may apply to 2018, 2019, and any subsequent years. Such an exercise, again as an example, would permit a fiduciary to take note that a particular long-term investment was likely to produce little or no accounting income but significant capital appreciation, and to provide accordingly for ongoing adjustments to occur as long as those conditions prevailed.[20]

While it still may be prudent to regularly review those conditions, "an announced commitment to a long-term strategy of adjustments might provide reassuring predictability and enhance the 'regularity of income' cited as a factor for consideration in Section 201(e)(4)."[21]

---

16. *Id.*
17. *Id.*
18. *Id.*
19. *Id.* at 26.
20. *Id.*
21. *Id.*

A California decision[22] addressed the question of whether a petition by a beneficiary to modify her share of the trust by adjusting between principal and income would violate a trust's no-contest clause. In this case, a decedent created an irrevocable trust with IBM stock. The trust had three tiers of beneficiaries, each with different interests. The first-tier beneficiaries were entitled to fixed monthly payments, with the balance of the trust income to be accumulated and added to principal. Upon the death of the last of the first-tier beneficiaries to die, the trust assets were to be divided into three equal shares, each administered as a separate trust for the benefit of the second-tier beneficiaries. The second-tier beneficiaries were entitled to net income and upon their deaths, it was to pass to their issue. If a second-tier beneficiary died without issue, the deceased beneficiary's share was to be divided into equal shares for his or her siblings or nieces or nephews. The third-tier beneficiaries were the children of two of the three second-tier beneficiaries.

The trust contained a no-contest clause that provided that no trust property was to be paid to a beneficiary who "has, *directly or indirectly*, alone or in cooperation or conjunction with others, *contested or sought to impair, object to or invalidate this declaration of trust* or any instrument whatsoever by which [the grantor] hereafter shall seek to add or cause to be added, assets to these trusts."[23] By 1992, the trust was worth $22 million and was generating more than $1.2 million of income each year for the benefit of the second-tier beneficiaries. By the end of 2004, the plaintiff (one of the second-tier beneficiaries) had a separate trust interest worth more than $11 million. The plaintiff in that year asked the trustee to adjust between the principal and income of the plaintiff's share, increasing the annual distribution to the plaintiff. The trustee wrote to both the plaintiff and to all known beneficiaries advising that he proposed to transfer over $130,000 from principal of the plaintiffs' trusts to income (which would then be distributed to the plaintiff). Because a number of beneficiaries objected, the trustee decided not to make the proposed adjustment and the plaintiff filed an application under California law to obtain a judicial determination as to whether her petition to adjust between principal and income would violate the no-contest clause. The plaintiff's explanation for the need for an adjustment was that, as a result of investing the trust assets in accordance with a total return objective, the investments generated insufficient income to provide the plaintiff with "that degree of beneficial enjoyment that she would ordinarily expect to receive as the sole income beneficiary of a separate trust for her benefit."[24] Over four years, the income distributed to her had dropped from $340,000 to $265,000. The plaintiff's adjustment request was not only for the year 2004 but was to be an ongoing strategy, under which she would receive a guaranteed minimum yield of 4

22. McKenzie v. Vanderpoel, 151 Cal. App. 4th 1442 (2007).
23. *Id.* at 1445–46.
24. *Id.* at 1448.

percent of her trust property each year. The third-tier beneficiaries opposed her application, claiming that the adjustment would impair the trust provisions and would constitute a contest under the no-contest clause.

The court addressed the plaintiff's various arguments. Most importantly, the plaintiff argued that she was merely invoking a statutory procedure for adjustment between principal and income, which cannot violate a no-contest clause. The court held that the "mere availability of the . . . procedure"[25] was not dispositive of the issue. The court next held that the adjustment petition is within the scope of the no-contest clause. The language of the no-contest clause, according to the court, applies to any attempt to "impair" the trust, and by using that term, the trustor intended that the clause would apply to circumstances broader than an attempt to invalidate the entire trust.

In summary, the court concluded that the "availability of a statutory procedure under [the California Uniform Principal and Income Act] to reallocate principal and income does not exempt the adjustment petition from the scope of the trust's no-contest clause."[26] The court also concluded that the adjustment petition would impair the trust by guaranteeing the plaintiff a minimum income and allowing the trustee to reallocate assets from principal that is to be reserved to the third-tier beneficiaries.

The significant point here is that, had the trustee itself requested and made the adjustment, there would have been no triggering of the no-contest clause. It seems inconsistent to state, on the one hand, that the trustee under the statutory adjustment power can decide to adjust or not without invoking adverse consequences, while the beneficiary (who is another party entitled to take advantage of the statutory provision) does. Nevertheless, following this case, it is important to bear in mind that any petition from a beneficiary that seeks to adjust between income and principal (or, presumably, to convert to a "unitrust") potentially could invoke a no-contest clause. This means that any such effort should be preceded by a request from the court that the petition requesting the adjustment will not trigger any no-contest clause in the trust agreement.

C. Conversion to a Unitrust

While the precise origin or intent of the word "unitrust" is not clear, a "unitrust" can be thought of as a trust in which there is a "unity" of interest between the current and remainder beneficiaries because both benefit from increasing values of the trust assets. It is a trust in which the distributions to the current beneficiaries are defined as percentages of the net value of trust assets rather than by the nature of the investment returns (i.e., "income" versus "principal"). Rather than trying to alter the definition of "income," as the power to adjust does, it sidesteps

25. *Id.* at 1452.
26. *Id.* at 1454.

the problem altogether. Because all unitrust beneficiaries benefit from rising trust asset values, the trustee is able to invest the assets for long-term growth to the benefit of all beneficiaries.

The IRS took up the question of whether and when an allocation between income and principal or a conversion to a unitrust will be respected (discussed in more detail later). Treasury Regulation section 1.643(b)-1 states, in part, that an allocation of amounts between income and principal pursuant to applicable local law will be respected if local law provides for a reasonable apportionment between the income and remainder beneficiaries of the total return of the trust for the year, including ordinary and tax-exempt income, capital gains, and appreciation. It also provides that a state statute providing that income is a unitrust amount of no less than 3 percent and no more than 5 percent of the fair market value of the trust assets, whether determined annually or averaged on a multiple-year basis, is a reasonable apportionment of the total return of the trust. The consequences of not having these allocations respected by the IRS include the recognition of gain to a beneficiary under Internal Revenue Code section 1001 or the treatment of the allocation of principal to income, for instance, as a taxable gift from the remainder beneficiary to the current beneficiary.

Following the issuance of these regulations and before the drafting of UFIPA, most state unitrust statutes limited unitrust conversions to these parameters in the Treasury Regulations—"a unitrust amount of no less than 3% and no more than 5% of the fair market value of the trust assets, whether determined annually or averaged on a multiple year basis."[27]

By contrast, article 3 of UFIPA is broader and more flexible than the laws of most states. It does not limit unitrust distribution percentages to the IRS-approved 3–5 percent range. For example, it allows the trustee to distribute a percentage of the trust assets' market value determined on the basis of a rolling average of values for periods other than years. The comment to article 3 mentions 12 quarters as an example. The benefit, according to the comment, is that this change to rolling averages "can reduce potential fluctuations in distributions caused by short-swing movements in the stock market. Although the rate of increase in the unitrust distribution to the current income beneficiary will lag the performance of the portfolio, the current income beneficiary will benefit in down years."[28] Article 3 of UFIPA also allows for the placement of a ceiling or floor on the unitrust payout amount or on the size of fluctuation of the unitrust amount from year to year or period to period. It even allows for a variable unitrust rate itself and different treatment for (or even exclusion from) different types of assets.

27. Treas. Reg. § 1.643(b)-1.

28. Uniform Fiduciary Income and Principal Act art. 3 cmt. at 31, Unif. L. Comm'n (2018), https://www.uniformlaws.org/HigherLogic/System/DownloadDocumentFile.ashx?DocumentFileKey=0f589496-fd89-29b5-7306-f9d0292e58d9&forceDialog=0.

If a trustee wants to use the safe harbor in the Treasury Regulations, section 309(b) limits the available drafting parameters for trusts that provide a "special tax benefit" (defined in UFIPA section 102(19)).

Section 301 includes several definitions applicable to unitrusts. Section 303 provides that a fiduciary, without court approval, may:

> (1) convert an income trust to a unitrust if the fiduciary adopts in a record a unitrust policy for the trust providing:
>
> > (A) that in administering the trust the net income of the trust will be a unitrust amount rather than net income determined without regard to this [article]; and
> >
> > (B) the percentage and method used to calculate the unitrust amount;
>
> (2) change the percentage or method used to calculate a unitrust amount for a unitrust if the fiduciary adopts in a record a unitrust policy or an amendment or replacement of a unitrust policy providing changes in the percentage or method used to calculate the unitrust amount; or
>
> (3) convert a unitrust to an income trust if the fiduciary adopts in a record a determination that, in administering the trust, the net income of the trust will be net income determined without regard to this [article] rather than a unitrust amount.[29]

Under section 303(b), in order to make one of these conversions, a fiduciary must determine that the action will assist the fiduciary to administer a trust impartially; must send "a notice in a record, in the manner required by Section 304, describing and proposing to take the action"[30] must send a copy of the notice to several listed parties; and must not receive, by the date specified in the notice, an objection in a record to the action proposed. If the fiduciary does receive an objection, the fiduciary or a beneficiary may request the court to have the proposed action "taken as proposed, taken with modifications, or prevented."[31] Sections 303(d)–(f) provide resolution for a fiduciary who decides not to take a proposed action or who is responding to a request by a beneficiary to do so. Section 304 provides details of the fiduciary's notice to beneficiaries.

Section 305 sets out the requirement for a "unitrust policy" that a trustee must adopt when administering a unitrust. This policy must provide

> (1) the unitrust rate or the method for determining the unitrust rate under Section 306;
>
> (2) the method for determining the applicable value under Section 307; and
>
> (3) the rules described in Sections 306 through 309 which apply in the administration of the unitrust, whether the rules are:

---

29. *Id.* § 303 at 34–35.
30. *Id.* at 35.
31. *Id.* at 36.

(A) mandatory, as provided in Sections 307(a) and 308(a); or

(B) optional, as provided in Sections 306, 307(b), 308(b), and 309(a), to the extent the fiduciary elects to adopt those rules.[32]

The determination of the unitrust rate is set forth in section 306 and provides the flexibility described earlier. Section 307 provides the method for determining an asset's fair market value and the "applicable value" (the amount to which the unitrust distribution percentage is applied). This method must be set forth in the unitrust policy. This section provides significantly more complexity than most existing state unitrust conversion statutes and is intended, according to the comment, to "counterbalance the effects of the market to provide a smoother and more predictable unitrust amount from year to year."[33]

Section 308 provides alternatives for the types of periods to be used, over which the calculation is made. As described earlier, it provides significant flexibility. Finally, section 309 sets out several different rules that can be applied to unitrusts, as well as the safe harbor rules for unitrusts that provide "a special tax benefit" or that have a fiduciary who is not an "independent person."

This brief description provides only an overview of the unitrust conversion provisions under section 303. They provide a great deal of flexibility, but at the cost of significant potential complexity. An attorney drafting unitrusts under these provisions will need to put a great deal of thought into their terms and must keep "records" of decisions made.

State law on unitrust conversions, though not yet applicable to UFIPA, is still sparse. A fairly simple New York decision[34] is the first recorded case in New York to deal with that state's statute allowing the conversion of an "income" trust to a unitrust. The only important aspect of this decision was the court's interpretation of the intent of the testator in creating the trust. The petitioner (the surviving spouse of the trustor) provided affidavits from herself, a remainder person of the trust, and the attorney who drafted the will. Because the trust was created in order to minimize estate taxes (which would not have occurred with an outright bequest) and because the trust gave the surviving spouse not only all of the income but a power of invasion for her support and maintenance in the standard of living to which she is accustomed, and because it was also clear that her income without the trust was insufficient to provide for current living expenses, the court decided that the primary intent of the trust was to benefit the surviving spouse. As a result of this determination, the court granted the petition to convert the trust to a unitrust.

This case is important more for its future ramifications than its actual result. The court determined that the trust was created for the primary benefit of the

32. *Id.* § 305 at 41–42.

33. *Id.* § 307 cmt. at 44.

34. *In re* Estate of Ives, 192 Misc. 2d 479 (Sur. Ct. 2002).

surviving spouse. Therefore, this determination could lead to the conclusion that the trustee could have invested trust assets to favor her over the remainder beneficiaries (for instance, by investing primarily in fixed-income investments that would guarantee an income stream but would not keep pace with inflation). In some cases this might be the appropriate result, while in others it may not (for example, if the children of the trustor came from a prior marriage). Therefore, this case is important not only because it shows a court trying to determine the intent behind the document but also because it shows that it is important for the drafter of a trust to include intent language wherever possible to assist a future court in that determination.

D. Impact of Treasury Regulations on Principal and Income Allocations

As mentioned earlier, the failure to have a principal or income adjustment or a unitrust conversion "recognized" by the IRS can have negative tax consequences. These rules apply to actions taken not only under UFIPA but also in any state. Under the Treasury Regulations, while trust provisions that depart fundamentally from "traditional principles of income and principal" generally are not recognized, "an allocation of amounts between income and principal pursuant to applicable local law will be respected if local law provides for a reasonable apportionment between the income and remainder beneficiaries of the total return of the trust for the year."[35] This "reasonable apportionment" takes two forms. First, "a state statute providing that income is a unitrust amount of no less than 3% and no more than 5% of the fair market value of the trust assets, whether determined annually or averaged on a multiple year basis, is a reasonable apportionment of the total return of the trust."[36] Second, a state statute "that permits the trustee to make adjustments between income and principal to fulfill the trustee's duty of impartiality between the income and remainder beneficiaries is generally a reasonable apportionment of the total return of the trust."[37]

Adjustments between income and principal or conversions to unitrusts, when authorized under state statute, are respected whether the distribution of income is mandatory or discretionary, regardless of the number of beneficiaries, and "regardless of which alternate permitted method is actually used."[38] Further, the trust complies "with all requirements of the state statute for switching methods" of determining income, and if the methods are authorized by state statute, then the switch does not constitute "a recognition event for purposes of section

35. Treas. Reg. § 1.643(b)-1.
36. *Id.*
37. *Id.*
38. *Id.*

1001 and will not result in a taxable gift from the trust's grantor or any of the trust's beneficiaries."[39]

Note, however, that if the methods of determining income are not specifically authorized by state statute but are valid under state law (including a switch via judicial decision or binding nonjudicial settlement), a switch *may* constitute a recognition event for purposes of section 1001 and *may* result in taxable gifts, "based on the relevant facts and circumstances."[40]

E. Judicial Determinations

A fiduciary, considering whether or not to take one of the actions described, may not feel comfortable taking actions on her own but may prefer to seek judicial approval for that action. Section 202 of UFIPA sets out the means of obtaining judicial review. This section was adapted from section 105 of the 1997 Act, but it expands the scope of actions covered beyond the power to adjust to include "fiduciary decisions" (described next). The comment states that "[s]ubsection (b) retains the general rule of Section 105(a) of the 1997 Act that a court will intervene only if it determines that the fiduciary decision was an abuse of the fiduciary's discretion. The statement that 'A fiduciary's decision is not an abuse of discretion merely because the court would have exercised the power in a different manner or would not have exercised the power,' although obviously true, is deleted as unnecessary."[41]

Section 202 defines "fiduciary decision" as

> (1) a fiduciary's allocation between income and principal or other determination regarding income and principal required or authorized by the terms of the trust or this [act];
>
> (2) the fiduciary's exercise or nonexercise of a discretionary power regarding income and principal granted by the terms of the trust or this [act], including the power to adjust under Section 203, convert an income trust to a unitrust under Section 303(a)(1), change the percentage or method used to calculate a unitrust amount under Section 303(a)(2), or convert a unitrust to an income trust under Section 303(a)(3); or
>
> (3) the fiduciary's implementation of a decision described in paragraph (1) or (2).[42]

39. *Id.*

40. *Id.*

41. Uniform Fiduciary Income and Principal Act § 202 cmt. at 20, Unif. L. Comm'n (2018), https://www.uniformlaws.org/HigherLogic/System/DownloadDocumentFile.ashx?DocumentFileKey=0f589496-fd89-29b5-7306-f9d0292e58d9&forceDialog=0.

42. *Id.* § 202 at 18–19.

F. Some Conclusions

As mentioned earlier, UFIPA is a relatively recent development and has yet to be adopted in most states. Presumably, the level of adoption will increase as professionals become more familiar with UFIPA. This chapter has not provided any detailed analysis of the act as a whole, nor has it provided any specific information about the acts adopted in different states. Rather, it has focused on those aspects of principal and income acts that have the most impact on trustee investing and that have been adopted in one form or another by most states. Given the differences among state principal and income acts, additional research is required by the attorney on these topics under the laws of the state in which the attorney practices.

13

Trust Drafting Suggestions

So far, this book has set out the law of trustee investments and the problems that can arise therefrom. We now turn to the ways in which trusts can be drafted to avoid such problems. The following is not a "form book"; creating specific language is the trade of the attorney. Instead, this chapter is intended to provide a starting point for the attorney to create a form book of her own. The chapter is divided into four categories: Purpose, Distributions, Beneficiary Control, Distributions, and Trust Protectors and Advisors. Each category describes an area of drafting that can make the process of trustee investing become more streamlined and (hopefully) easier to execute. Each category will contain drafting suggestions an attorney might consider.

A. Purpose

Purpose in a document gives the beneficiaries and trustee knowledge about why the trust exists. Failure to define purpose can be a serious drafting flaw because it allows the beneficiary (who is also a child of the grantor) to argue over what a parent really wanted the beneficiary to have. However, even though we might recognize its importance, most drafters still don't seem to use "purpose" language.

The problem of not defining "purpose has been recognized for a long time. For example, over 60 years ago, the Oregon Supreme Court noted that

> [t]he difficulty in many if not most of these [abuse of trustee discretion] cases is finding the purpose of the settlor with sufficient definiteness to be helpful . . . . The settlor's specific design in framing a discretionary trust is normally unexpressed or vaguely outlined.[1]

Two years later, Professor Edward C. Halbach, Jr., repeated those sentiments:

> [t]oo frequently trust instruments provide no guidance as to the purpose and scope of the [discretionary] power. Although determining and assisting in

1. Rowe v. Rowe, 219 Or. 599, 606 (1959).

the formulation of the donor's intentions is a primary counseling function, it is apparently one of the most neglected aspects of estate planning. A poorly defined discretionary power often results.[2]

From the author's perspective, as one who reviews daily various estate-planning documents, the situation has not improved all these years later. So how should purpose be addressed in a trust?

1. Determine "Protection"

To begin with, the only reason trusts are put in place is to protect one or more people from one or more other people. The universe of protection can be broken down into four categories:

- Protect beneficiaries from themselves (minors, spendthrifts, those with special needs)
- Protect beneficiaries against creditors (including future ex-spouses)
- Protect beneficiaries against each other (kids from a prior marriage vs. the second spouse)
- Protect beneficiaries from the IRS

Identifying with the client the thing that they are protecting beneficiaries from will go a long way to identifying the real purpose of the trust. For example, if a trust is designed to protect a beneficiary from himself, that beneficiary may not be given the ability to provide input into trustee investments. On the other hand, if the trust is designed to protect a beneficiary from the IRS (e.g., the trust is put in place solely for tax planning), such input might be very helpful in easing the trustee/beneficiary relationship.

Drafting Suggestion: Start the drafting process by finding out who the client is trying to protect and from what. This is more of an interview technique than a drafting one, but if an attorney starts here, the rest of the suggestions discussed next lay out much more easily.

2. General Purpose

Following the "protection" discussion, the attorney and client are ready to set out the primary purpose of the trust in the agreement. Such general language is useful in all aspects of trust administration. In the case of trustee investing, purpose language tells the trustee why the trust was created, which in turn provides the trustee with some direction as to how the trust assets should be invested.

Drafting Suggestion: Add general purpose language to *all* trusts. Regardless of the purpose for which it is intended, any trust can benefit from a clear statement of the grantor's intent. This is the area of drafting most overlooked by

2. Edward C. Halbach Jr., *Problems of Discretion in Discretionary Trusts*, 61 COLUM. L. REV. 1424, 1434 (1961).

lawyers and also the most critical to the success of a trust administration. Such language should be included in a separate paragraph, so that there is no risk of a trustee or the court confusing precatory purpose language with distribution language.

3. Beneficiary Preference

One particular aspect of trust purpose requires particular attention. Very few trust agreements specify which beneficiaries, if any, should be preferred over others. Is this a trust primarily for the benefit of the current or remainder beneficiaries? Should one class be favored over another? Although this is sometimes very hard for a grantor to deal with, if such expressions of preference were used more frequently, many trust disputes would be resolved more quickly.

Knowing which beneficiaries should be preferred over others may help a trustee determine asset allocation. For example, if the "primary" beneficiary has a short life expectancy, the trustee might invest more conservatively (e.g., invest more heavily in bonds) than the trustee otherwise might do. But the trustee does not have this flexibility if a primary beneficiary isn't identified in the document.

Drafting Suggestion: Add beneficiary preference language to *all* trusts.

B. Beneficiary Control

Trusts are all about control: who has it and who doesn't. Research suggests that control over one's own circumstances leads to greater happiness. The opposite is also true. When people lack control over a thing, they tend to become cynical about it and withdraw. Our clients often come to us feeling a lack of control: over their finances, the state of the tax law, their kids' futures, everything. "Control" has many different connotations, not all of them positive. Control can be defined in three different ways. First, there is control of external things (like controlling others through rewards or punishment). Second, there is internal control over our assets, attitudes, and outlook. Finally, knowledge is a third type of control.

Internal control over one's own circumstances is beneficial. One of the most famous happiness studies tracked the journals of 180 nuns, all of whom were born before 1917. When in their 20s, the nuns were asked to write down autobiographical journal entries. Fifty years later, researchers coded the entries for positive emotional content. It turned out that the nuns whose entries were more positive lived nearly ten years longer than those whose entries were negative or neutral. In fact, by age 85, 90 percent of the happiest quartile of nuns were still alive, as compared to only 34 percent of the least happy quartile.[3] One sweeping study indicated that employees who felt they had little control over deadlines

3. Shawn Achor, The Happiness Advantage 42 (2010).

imposed by others had a 50 percent higher rate of coronary heart disease than their counterparts. In a study of the elderly, a group of nursing home residents who were given more control over simple daily tasks, like being in charge of their own house plants, not only became happier but also cut their mortality rate in half.[4]

Finally, if a person has sufficient information about a process or outcome so that he can respond based on that knowledge, then he has at least a feeling of control. This third type of control indicates that one's involvement, even if it is only to be fully informed and without any actual control, can be empowering.

So how can control impact trust drafting? For starters, the beneficiary might be given the power to remove and replace the trustee. This power makes the beneficiary feel like she has more control over her own destiny and (in the author's experience at least) leads to a better relationship with the trustee.

Drafting Suggestion: (Almost) always give beneficiaries the power to remove and replace trustees. The interesting thing is that, in most cases, if a beneficiary knows that he has this power, the beneficiary tends not to use it. Knowing that he has some level of control creates a sense of calm about problems that may arise with the trustee and tends to enable the beneficiary to arrive at a compromise regarding that problem.

Like any rule of thumb, this is a generalization. Of course some beneficiaries should not have this power. Of course some beneficiaries will be unhappy no matter what. But the ability to remove and replace trustees should be the rule, not the exception.

Drafting Suggestion: Consider giving beneficiaries veto power over selling special assets, along with intent language.

If a grantor funds a trust with an asset that has a special connection with the family (a business, a vacation home, income-producing real estate), the trustee is always in a dilemma: should the trustee sell the asset in order to comply with its duty to diversify? Giving beneficiaries the veto power over sale (rather than having a party like a trust protector or advisor govern such decisions) accomplishes two goals. First, it gives the beneficiaries greater control over trust assets, which we've already established is a good thing. Second, it eliminates the confusion over where fiduciary duty lies. The trustee is in charge of all assets but cannot sell a special asset if all or a majority of adult trustees object. Adding such a veto power is best done in conjunction with precatory language about the purpose of the trust being to hold the special asset and also a provision eliminating the duty to diversify with respect to this asset.

4. *Id.* at 132.

C. Distributions

Trust distribution provisions can be divided into two large subsets: objective and subjective. Since the only provisions that most beneficiaries care about are those that deal with what they get and when, reviewing the pros and cons of these two types with clients is very useful. They also greatly influence the way the trust assets are invested.

1. Objective Terms

There are generally two groups of objective trust terms: income-based and incentive-based. The income-based terms are the traditional group most estate planners are familiar with; under this model a beneficiary is entitled to all the income from the trust. There are a couple of modern offshoots, the unitrust and the adjustment between principal and income. Both, however, are based on the traditional notion of "all income" but with modifications to take into account the mandates of modern portfolio theory.

The second group, incentive trusts, has increased dramatically in popularity over the past 20 years. Such provisions have some superficial appeal and (at least in the case of drug testing) may be critical in caring for a beneficiary. They encourage or discourage positive or negative beneficiary behaviors. They are also easy to administer: show me your W-2 and I give you the money, pass your drug test and I give you the money. They leave no room for a trustee to be overindulgent.

However, objective provisions also have serious problems. The traditional "income only" provisions are virtually useless in most settings, because they bear no relation to any goals that the grantor might have. The income might be too much or too little for the purposes for which the trust was created. The same is true for unitrusts and for income with the trustee ability to adjust between principal and income: neither relates to real-world client goals for the beneficiary. They are as often as not shorthand solutions suggested by the drafter.

One variant of the "income" model has some relevance to real-world goals, and that is the dollar amount, adjusted for inflation. For instance, the beneficiary is to receive $100,000 per year, adjusted for inflation. This type of provision allows the grantor to establish a standard of living by creating essentially a salary from the trust. Inflation adjustment is obviously critical in this context to ensure that the beneficiary does not lose ground to inflation over time. Note that, even in those cases when an "all income" provision is required (e.g., in the case of QTIP trusts), a "greater of" provision can be used (i.e., the beneficiary shall be entitled to the greater of all net income or the inflation-adjusted dollar amount).

Further, objective provisions, which are fundamentally restrictive, do not allow for changing circumstances. The beneficiary who develops a debilitating illness that prevents her from earning at prior levels, for example, may find herself impoverished if the trust is not drafted broadly enough. In a more general sense, anyone who drafts a long-term trust with specific, objective terms, believing he knows what the world will look like 20 or 50 years from now, is probably thinking too narrowly.

2. Subjective Terms

Subjective provisions are those that require the exercise of discretion by the trustee in making certain value judgments. The subjective standard most attorneys are familiar with is the trustee's ability to distribute principal for "health, education, maintenance, and support." The trustee must decide what constitutes "support," for example. This flexibility is seen by many as a significant benefit. However, if a discretionary trust is to be used, several additional provisions should be added. First, the grantor should give clear guidance as to the exercise of the discretion. Further, trustee exculpation should be added, including perhaps provisions that set forth how the costs of litigation are to be paid (such costs may be assessed against the beneficiary who brought it, for example). These measures will ensure that the trustee will exercise discretion in a manner as close as possible to that the grantor intended and may do so with less fear that he will be sued for doing so. Finally, even if such provisions are added, some problems remain. First, the more discretion given to the trustee, the greater the likelihood that the trustee will exercise it in a manner the grantor would not have agreed with. Second, discretion guarantees only flexibility, not success.

Drafting Suggestion: Don't use "all income" when defining a beneficiary's distribution rights. There are few habits in trust drafting as automatic and yet counterproductive as giving a beneficiary "all income." Excluding the few times when it is required (e.g., in QTIP trusts), there is no reason to give a beneficiary all income (and even then a better solution can be found, like using a "greater of income or . . ." standard). It has little relation to real-world goals and pits beneficiaries against each other, because the trustee's investment choices benefit one beneficiary over another.

Drafting Suggestion: Consider an inflation-adjusted dollar amount. If "all income" is the most overused distribution provision, the most underused is the inflation-adjusted dollar amount (e.g., "beneficiary shall receive $75,000 per year, increased in each year by consumer price index "). No client knows how much "all income" will buy in the future, but everyone knows how much $75,000 per year in today's dollars will buy. Using this standard makes principal distributions easier to draft as well, because there will be less need for "support" or "maintenance" if a minimum standard has been applied.

Drafting Suggestion: Consider a unitrust. If the inflation-adjusted dollar amount is too radical for you, at least consider the unitrust distribution. This has two benefits over "all income": the trustee can invest for total return and not income production, and the percentage can be fine-tuned more than "income" can.

Drafting Suggestion: Add "standards" preferences to all trusts. A great many, probably most, irrevocable trusts allow for distributions of principal for a beneficiary's "health, education, maintenance, and support." However, not all of these standards necessarily are created equal. Is education more important than other purposes, for example? Clarity about standards is not often included, but many grantors do have strong feelings about priority. This tip is especially useful with the inflation-adjusted dollar amount. In that case, education and medical care would likely be emphasized over support or maintenance.

Drafting Suggestion: Be more specific about what the standards mean. For instance, paying for a beneficiary's support can often be contrary to the grantor's objectives (most grantors want their beneficiaries to be productive). Of course, there are plenty of circumstances in which support is appropriate (e.g., when a beneficiary is attending college or for a surviving spouse who has spent her life working in the home). Distributions for "health" might be expanded to be clear that the trustee can pay insurance premiums and perhaps also reimburse employee copays for such insurance, insurance premiums for disability, accidental death , and perhaps even long-term care or life insurance designed to replace the income of the working spouse in the event of her death (being mindful, of course, not to create any "incidence of ownership" problems).

D. Trust Protectors and Advisors

One of the most popular recent topics in estate planning has been the use of trust protectors and advisors.[5] The argument for using them is that they can provide greater flexibility to accommodate changes in beneficiary circumstance and oversee trustee behavior and do so without generating the cost of court proceedings.[6] Overseeing trust investments is a very common use for such decision-makers.

However, there are problems with using such decision-makers. For example, the terminology itself is confusing, as the terms "trust protector" and "trust advisor" are often used interchangeably.[7] It can be argued, however, that they are different, as a trust protector tends to be the holder of a power, while a trust advisor tends to have the power to control or constrain a trustee. Maintaining this distinction may be useful for the drafter and the client.

Of much more importance is the unresolved question of fiduciary duty and whether the document or state law effectively can eliminate such a duty altogether. If those duties can be completely eliminated, where does the fiduciary duty lie, if anywhere? If a trustee's fiduciary duty is trumped by a person with no such duty, where does that leave the beneficiaries? Many commentators and even some state laws seem to believe that those duties can be eliminated, even though

5. *See, e.g.*, Alexander A. Bove, Jr., *The Case against the Trust Protector*, 37 ACTEC L.J. 77 (2011).
6. *Id.*
7. *Id.* at 78.

the Restatement (Third) of Trusts and the Uniform Trust Code both indicate that a nonbeneficiary holding a trust power is presumed to be a fiduciary.[8]

This "obsession" with exculpating trust protectors from liability for breach of fiduciary duty is perhaps the original product of those who drafted and promoted offshore asset protection trusts,[9] even though subsequent offshore cases involving the question of whether a trust protector is a fiduciary seem to say that they are.[10] At least one commentator has opined that

> there is little question that if the "drafted-away" duty is breached by a disinterested protector who is deemed to be a fiduciary and a claim is made, the particular state law exculpating the protector would have to be struck down by a court.[11]

Further, faced with a decision made by a nonfiduciary trust protector that would be considered a breach of duty if made by a trustee, it is also quite likely that a court would go out of its way to find that some kind of minimum standard exists, regardless of the document or state law.

In light of these concerns, at least one important commentator has said that, except in enumerated circumstances, "most trusts do NOT need a trust advisor or trust protector."[12] A trust advisor or protector is best added to address specific needs in specific circumstances. Obviously one such specific need is to manage investments generally or only specific investments (like a closely held business).

Drafting Suggestion: Be clear about whether the decision-maker is a "trust advisor" or a "trust protector." A useful distinction is between "trust advisors," who should be considered the persons "to whom one or more powers are given to direct the trustee in carrying out the trustee's traditional trustee duties," and "trust protectors," the persons "to whom one or more powers have been given that relate to one or more specific trust matters but do not involve or infringe on the trustee's performance of traditional trustee duties."[13] Under this approach, a trust advisor may be responsible for participating in investment decisions, for example, while trust protectors may be responsible for things like changing trust situs.

Drafting Suggestion: Carefully limit the scope of a decision-maker's duties. This can come in two forms. First, limit all third-party decision-makers to powers and duties that are specifically enumerated in the document. The trust agreement should spell out that those parties have *only* those powers specifically included, with no additional powers being implied.[14] Second, consider giving

8. *Id.* at 82.

9. *Id.* at 84.

10. *Id.* at 85.

11. *Id.* at 83.

12. Kathleen R. Sherby, *In Protectors We Trust: The Nature and Effective Use of "Trust Protectors" as Third Party Decision Makers*, 49TH ANN. HECKERLING INST. ON EST. PLAN. ch. 15, ¶ 1508.1 (2015).

13. *Id.* ¶ 1501.2.

14. *Id.* ¶ 1508.4.

third-party decision-makers only the power to veto a trustee's decisions, rather than independent decision-making authority. While not perfect for every situation, thinking about it in these terms limits the scope of the third party's power, especially if that third party is not being held to a fiduciary standard.

14

Developing the Investment Plan

This chapter addresses the drafting and implementation of a written investment plan. As discussed earlier, UPIA section 8 provides that the adequacy of a fiduciary's investment performance will be based not upon his actual investment returns but rather the appropriateness of the investment plan that he constructs. Drafting the investment plan is the personal responsibility of the trustee and can't be delegated. Further, the case law has demonstrated that consistent beneficiary communication will go a long way to relieving a trustee of potential liability for loss in investments. Therefore, a written investment plan that takes into account the specific situation of the trust terms agreement and the beneficiaries' specific situations is the most important piece of protection a trustee can have.

Corporate fiduciaries have, as a matter of course, systems in place to establish a written investment plan (although, as the case law points out, even those written investment plans are not foolproof). Therefore, this chapter is aimed at the individual trustee and her advisors.

A. Investment Plans Generally

Developing a successful investment plan is easier if the following steps are taken:

- First, review the document.
- Second, determine the particular situations of the current and remainder beneficiaries.
- Third, determine the transfer and income tax consequences of the particular trust.
- Fourth, based on all of that information, develop the investment strategy.
- Fifth, review the original assets, based on that investment strategy.

The following text will discuss each of these steps in greater detail.

1. Review the Document

This first step, though it seems self-evident and simple, can cause trouble. First, is the trustee "directed" or merely "authorized" to hold a concentrated position in a single asset? As the Restatement makes clear, mere authorization alone will not relieve the trustee of liability if he holds that concentrated position and the trust property drops in value. Second, as the *Dumont* case makes painfully clear, a trustee should be very careful to distinguish precatory language from mandatory. Making such a distinction is not always simple, and the trustee should not jump to any quick conclusions. When in doubt, a trustee should consider consulting the drafting attorney, if she is still in practice, to help with the interpretation. Note, however, that this is only a first step. A trustee cannot simply rely on the word of the drafter that a provision is mandatory or precatory if the plain language provides otherwise.

In doubtful cases, the trustee has three alternatives: first, he can simply rely on his own interpretation and hope that it is not challenged later; second, he can make a determination that a particular direction is either mandatory or precatory and then confirm that interpretation with the beneficiaries before proceeding; or third, he can petition a court for instructions interpreting the language. All three of these options contain some risk; a trustee who acts alone has the greatest liability exposure, a trustee who seeks beneficiary approval may not obtain it, and a trustee who petitions the court for instructions risks angering the beneficiaries by incurring additional cost and may not obtain the answer he seeks (or indeed any answer at all). In general, the best approach of the three is probably to consult with the beneficiaries. If they disagree with the trustee's interpretation, the trustee can then pursue the court instructions with a greater likelihood of success because there is now an actual dispute among the parties.

After looking at the trust agreement itself, the trustee can look at other facts surrounding the trust's creation. Gift tax returns also may be helpful. For example, if a return indicates that generation-skipping transfer tax exemption was allocated to a trust, it probably indicates that the investment time horizon is a long one. However, it is important not to rely solely on such returns; even if a return shows no GST exemption allocated to a trust, the automatic allocation rules may have applied to accomplish the same result. Finally, if the settlor is still alive, the trustee should seek a written statement of intent from the settlor herself.

2. Determine the Beneficiaries' Situation

Once the trust has been reviewed, the trustee should decide what the needs of the primary and secondary beneficiaries are. Identifying a beneficiary as "primary" or "secondary" is a subjective determination (unless, as discussed earlier, the drafting lawyer has spelled out those roles in the agreement), but the circumstances surrounding the creation of the trust can help in making that determination. The relative economic position of the beneficiaries also may help in this determination. If the income beneficiary has few assets of her own, then that beneficiary may be the primary one. If that beneficiary has significant assets outside the trust, however, she may be a secondary beneficiary.

Another fact to consider is the size of the trust. If the value of the trust assets is significant and the trust produces more than enough return for the income beneficiary, then the trustee would be justified in pursuing a more aggressive growth strategy. On the other hand, if the value of the trust's assets is not significant, the trustee may take a more conservative stance.

Consider, for example, a trust that is created for the lifetime support of a surviving spouse, with the remainder interest passing to the children from a prior marriage. This fairly common situation presents a complex and conflicting set of interests that the investment portfolio should consider. The trust investments not only must produce a sufficient return and adequate distributions to provide for the surviving spouse's support but also must not (to the extent possible) lose value to inflation.

Notice that circumstances will change the approach used. If the spouse has sufficient wealth for his own support and the beneficiaries are all getting along, the trustee may with everyone's approval invest primarily for growth and decide (with the spouse's approval, typically) not to generate much if any income. If the spouse needs the cash flow from the trust but the trust is of significant size, then the trustee may still choose to invest for growth but with some portion invested in income-producing assets sufficient to meet the spouse's needs. If the spouse needs the cash flow and the trust assets are more modest in size, the trustee may still decide to invest primarily for growth while simultaneously using either a unitrust conversion or an adjustment between principal and income as provided under the state's principal and income act. Each of these approaches has subtle but very important differences in approach.

This determination is a particularly sensitive one in this situation, because often the surviving spouse and the children from the prior marriage are not on the best of terms, and the decisions of the trustee will be scrutinized by all parties.

3. Determine the Tax Consequences

There are several different sets of tax consequence that can influence investment decisions. The presence of significant transfer tax liabilities on the death of a beneficiary may indicate that the trust should have a shorter time horizon, while the absence of such liabilities may indicate a longer one. So, for example, a QTIP trust will be taxed at the death of the surviving spouse, while a credit shelter trust should not be. This would indicate two different investment strategies for the trusts, even though the current beneficiary (and perhaps the distribution terms as well) is the same for both. It may be that the QTIP trust is invested to produce more income and less growth, while the credit shelter trust might be invested for more growth and little income production. This will also be the case where a nonspouse beneficiary has a general power of appointment, such that the trust assets will be included in the beneficiary's estate at death under Internal Revenue Code section 2041.

Another tax factor that already was mentioned is the question of whether GST exemption has been allocated to the trust. This would be the case, for example, in a "dynasty" trust, the purpose of which is to benefit many generations. Allocation of exemption is an indication (though not conclusive) that the trust is intended to have a long-term investment horizon.

4. Develop the Investment Strategy

The next step is to determine the level of risk the trustee needs to assume in order to meet the return expectations the trustee has established. This risk/reward analysis is central to the trustee's obligations under the UPIA. When making this determination, the trustee will need to consider the return objectives and the time horizon for investment of the particular trust.

At this point, the trustee should consider seeking professional guidance from an investment advisor if the trustee does not feel up to the tasks described. Given the mandates of the UPIA, a trustee is not free to ignore risk and return analysis and determination of trust purpose simply because she is unsophisticated. Since the UPIA allows a trustee to delegate investment responsibilities, not to do so could be viewed as a breach of trust.

The trustee next should select asset classes that are consistent with the expected return, the level of risk assumed, and the investment time horizon. Determining these asset classes may involve working around assets that the trustee is required to hold as the result of requirements in the trust agreement. For example, if the trustee is directed to hold as a significant portion of the trust assets stock in a closely held company, the trustee must determine how to build a portfolio of particular asset classes around that significant investment so that the goals of the trust can be achieved.

Once this investment policy statement is drafted, it should be circulated to all of the beneficiaries who otherwise would be entitled to an accounting. In the absence of any state statute that requires that such information be provided to certain beneficiaries, a good rule of thumb would be that such information, at a minimum, should be supplied to all vested beneficiaries (or their legal representatives). Further, a trustee should never consider that distributing this information one time only is adequate. Rather, the trustee should recirculate this investment policy statement annually, even if nothing has changed, to ensure that the beneficiaries are regularly reminded of its aims and have the opportunity to object to those aims.

5. Review Original Assets

Now that the trustee has a written investment strategy, the trustee must look at all the assets she has received and determine whether those assets are consistent with the mandates of that written strategy. For example, assume a client died owning a house and a $4 million bond portfolio. Assume also that the client's estate plan mandates that all trust assets pass to a credit shelter trust and to a QTIP trust, each with identical terms and each funded with $2 million. Finally, assume that the surviving spouse is a healthy 55-year-old with a 30-year life expectancy. Given that these trusts seem to be created for the primary benefit of the surviving spouse, and therefore that the trusts probably will have a long time horizon, the investments must assume some amount of risk to avoid losing ground to inflation over that time. This means that some portion of the bond portfolio (perhaps 50 or 60 percent) will have to be sold in order to invest in riskier assets that will generate a higher return over time (probably stocks). It will not be an adequate reason to retain all bonds that the grantor was naturally cautious and hated the idea of investing in stocks. Such information (unless codified in the agreement in the form of an investment statement or direction) is simply irrelevant.

B. Implementing the Investment Policy Statement

Once the statement has been formulated and circulated, the trustee must then follow its principles. If a detailed investment policy statement is formulated, the implementation step will be relatively simple; it will involve following all of the instructions in the statement. On the other hand, if the investment policy is of a more general nature, the trustee at the implementation level must decide which professional advisors to hire and which investment vehicles are appropriate for the size of the portfolio (this involves determining whether the level of expense of a managed fund is appropriate, as opposed to the lowered cost of indexed mutual funds). The implementation step also involves continued due diligence in selecting service providers, including money managers and asset custodians.

The trustee also must ensure that the goals set forth in the policy statement are followed and that they remain appropriate over time. This ongoing monitoring process also involves regularly checking on the level of expenses incurred in making investments, the performance of investment managers if active managers are used, the ongoing needs of the beneficiaries, and the rebalancing on a regular basis of investments to ensure that the balance originally pursued is maintained. These last two objectives often may prove to be the most difficult. First, balancing is necessary when one asset class outperforms another. For example, technology stocks in the late 1990s outperformed not only bonds but also other stocks. It took a very disciplined investor to rebalance his portfolio by selling off enough of the high-flying stocks to ensure that those stocks did not start to constitute a larger portion of the portfolio. Because rebalancing essentially means selling off some of the winners to invest more in the underperformers, it often goes against human nature.

Perhaps the most important aspect of monitoring, however, involves monitoring the needs of the beneficiaries. For example, if the trustee determines that a trust has been created for the primary benefit of an elderly beneficiary, and that elderly beneficiary has ever-increasing needs due to increased medical costs, then the trustee may need to revisit the investment policy statement to determine whether it needs to be revised to take these new facts into account. Finally, the monitoring and supervision stage will include the monitoring even of assets that are required to be held under the terms of the trust. A careful trustee will not hide behind a mandate that it hold a single high concentration of one stock, for example. Rather, that trustee will continue to monitor that single investment's performance, will continue to communicate with the beneficiaries about the ongoing prudence of this investment, and, if the beneficiaries cannot agree on its continued prudence, should seek instructions from the court of competent jurisdiction authorizing the trustee to continue to hold this high concentration of a single asset.

C. Applying the Plan in Special Circumstances

Drafting and implementing an investment policy statement can become even more complicated in the case of particular types of trusts or circumstances. For example, trusts designed to hold life insurance or high concentrations of a single asset can cause headaches. This section will look at those two situations and apply to them the analysis set forth earlier.

1. Irrevocable Life Insurance Trusts[1]

Irrevocable life insurance trusts (ILITs) raise a number of unique administration issues. Add to that the fact that many (if not most) ILITs are promoted at least initially by insurance professionals rather than lawyers, and you have the potential for a lot of problems.

Perhaps the most significant problem is the fact that the ILIT trustee often has no say in the type of policy, or the amount of premium, that is to be transferred to or paid by the trustee. In an ideal world, a trustee would have the flexibility to make all the appropriate decisions after taking enough time to work up the necessary analysis. Often, however, this is a luxury the trustee does not

1. Significant portions of this section were taken from Christopher P. Cline and Barry D. Flagg, "The Prudent Investor and Trust-Owned Life Insurance," a three-part article published in *ABA Trust & Investments* (Jan./Feb. 2007, Mar./Apr. 2007, and May/June 2007).

have. As a result, this section will discuss both the "ideal" approach (when the trustee is able to undertake such due diligence) and the "necessary" approach (when the trustee is not). It will discuss the five steps (first, review the document; second, determine the particular situations of the current and remainder beneficiaries; third, determine the transfer and income tax consequences of the particular trust; fourth, based on all of that information, develop the investment strategy; and fifth, review the original assets, based on that investment strategy) as they apply to ILITs and then will discuss the "necessary" approach, to be used when the five steps can't be applied.

a. Review the Document

The document review for ILITs mainly involves determining the trust purpose. At first glance, this may seem to be a silly step: the purpose is to hold life insurance! However, not all ILITs or policies are created equal. Perhaps the most important factor in determining the trust purpose is the time horizon. For example, an ILIT that is intended to pay estate taxes might hold a different type of policy, depending upon the insured's age. And it may be that the purpose has changed; with rising estate tax exemptions, ILITs that once were created for estate tax savings may no longer be necessary for that purpose. In that case, the trustee may want to exchange one type of policy (say a current whole life policy) for another (perhaps a variable product with a higher investment return potential) or simply terminate the policy altogether.

b. Determine the Beneficiaries' Situations

This is less of an immediate need, because the ILIT's purpose will usually be simply to make sure the policy stays in force. So this step might be devoted to the mechanics of the trust and specifically the "Crummey" withdrawal provisions. How are withdrawal notices to be delivered? If there are minors, to whom will notice be sent? Is the withdrawal right automatic, or is the trust drafted so that the trustee needs to get a notice from the donor before a donee has a withdrawal right?

Another issue that can surprise people is the payment of trustee fees. These fees must be paid from trust assets, and therefore the annual contribution by the grantor (and perhaps her spouse) should be calculated based on both the annual insurance premium needed and the fees that are due. This typically will be the case with a corporate trustee rather than an individual (in the author's experience, most ILIT trustees are friends or family members of the grantor and therefore tend to serve without pay).

c. Determine the Transfer and Income Tax Consequences

This is another point that, at first blush, doesn't seem significant, because the point of an ILIT usually is to ensure that the death benefit passes to trust beneficiaries without estate tax inclusion to the grantor. So the trust should be reviewed from that perspective, making sure that the insured will have no Internal Revenue Code section 2042 ownership ties to the trust policy and that there are no other estate tax "hooks" from the grantor's perspective.

The bigger question here may be whether the trust assets will be included in the beneficiary's taxable estate. This may be the case, for example, when the trust is not designed to last beyond the insured's death. The trustee also should determine whether or not GST tax exemption is automatically being allocated to the trust transfers. The trustee will need to ensure that such exemption is being allocated properly.

d. Develop the Investment Strategy

This is a much more difficult job, in many respects, than it is with other trusts because the strategy chosen is largely based on the insurance product selected. Given that the nature of most insurance products is to be confusing to most estate planning professionals, and completely mystifying to most clients, this can be a difficult step.

First, the strategy involves selecting the right type of insurance (term, whole, universal, variable). This step obviously involves working with the client's insurance agent as early in the process as possible so that he is aware of the process needed by the trustee. If the purpose of the ILIT is to cover estate tax costs, a younger insured might choose to buy a 20-year level term policy and "invest the difference," so that when the 20-year period has expired, the trust holds adequate liquid assets that the insurance is no longer needed. Alternatively, a variable product might be chosen so that the cash value builds inside the policy. On the other hand, an older insured might need the certainty of a whole life policy because her only asset is an interest in her closely held business, and term is too expensive.

After the policy is selected, the strength of the product needs to be reviewed, in terms of not only the strength of the issuing company but also the appropriateness of the premium amount and the policy's expenses. This step is certainly the most complex and may very well require the services of an expert, rather than simply relying on the representations of the agent selling the product. ILIT trustees should consider seeking advice with respect to a given policy's financial strength and claims-paying ability (i.e., default risk), cost competitiveness, pricing stability, cash value liquidity, and historical performance of invested assets.

Regardless of how the investigation is conducted, however, ILIT trustees must dig deeper than reviewing illustrations when determining the reasonableness of investment performance and the appropriateness of policy expenses. For instance, because illustrations show projected results based on combined investment and expense assumptions, they fail to provide trustees with specific information about expected returns, costs of insurance, cash-value-based "wrap fees," and premium loads that is necessary to justify policy expenses. In addition, because illustrations are generally only provided to agents licensed with a limited number of insurers, comparing illustrations provides the ILIT trustee with only a fraction of the comparative data.

e. Reviewing Original Assets and Conducting Annual Checkups

In a perfect world, the trustee will not need to review original assets because the trustee has been involved in the process of selecting that asset. At that point, the trustee is able to manage trust assets in a manner that maximizes benefits and minimizes costs. Such management occurs when the ILIT trustee defines portfolio objectives, continually measures the policy's pricing and performance, identifies the policy's strengths and weaknesses, investigates available alternative products, and makes necessary changes to the portfolio stemming from this information.

Further, if the objective of the ILIT is to provide a defined death benefit (for instance, to finance an obligation like buy-sell agreement funding or estate tax liabilities), the trustee also must ensure that planned premiums and corresponding cash values are adequate to pay future policy expenses until the policy matures at the insured's death. The trustee can do so by periodically measuring actual policy cash values against cash value targets from the original illustration of hypothetical policy values.

Regardless of the steps taken, however, a trustee cannot simply receive annual distributions from the grantor, pay the premiums, and be done. At a minimum, the trustee should be receiving in-force illustrations no less than once every other year to ensure that the product is performing as it was designed to do.

f. If All Else Fails: The Necessary Approach

While a discussion of the standards an ILIT trustee should strive for is all very interesting, it does not address the most common scenario. Typically, a client comes to the proposed ILIT trustee with the proposal already laid out and the product already selected. The plan already has been formulated by the agent selling the policy (or perhaps the lawyer who suggested the ILIT), and the trustee finds itself in a take-it-or-leave-it situation. While the trustee would like to take the steps just outlined, it does not have that option. Under these circumstances, the trustee's options are limited. The steps, in this case, are probably as follows:

- First, determine whether the trustee has the opportunity to make suggestions as to the type of policy chosen. If this opportunity is available, then determine the trust purpose and investment plan as described earlier. The trustee may not be able to apply the analysis regarding the pricing of the selected policy relative to those issued by other carriers, because the agent selling the policy may offer products from only a limited number of carriers. In this case, obtain a written instruction (hopefully with a written indemnification or hold-harmless agreement) from the grantor regarding the particular policy held.

- Second, if the trustee has no opportunity to suggest the type of policy used, the trustee should determine the trust purpose and the investment plan as described earlier. However, in this case, the investment plan should include a direction from the grantor to hold the policy presented (again, hopefully with an indemnification). The written instruction from the grantor should comply with the Prudent Investor Act's exception to the duty to diversify for "special assets"—assets with a special relation to the grantor.
- Finally, once the policy and the trust are in place and the premiums are being paid, the trustee should conduct the ongoing annual maintenance described earlier, including obtaining regular in-force illustrations from the agent as well as Monte Carlo simulations, if possible, to determine the likelihood of policy lapse. If this likelihood reaches an unacceptably high level, the trustee has the duty to advise the grantor or the beneficiaries that a tax-free exchange into another policy may be appropriate.

2. Special Circumstances: Large Concentrations

Another difficult situation is the trustee who is presented with a large concentration of trust assets held in a single investment. Rather than walk through the steps outlined earlier in a different way, the trustee should undertake those steps just as the trustee would with any trust and also should consider the following:

- The duty to diversify is not mandatory, it is merely a default. Particular circumstances such as the age or economic condition of one or more of the beneficiaries, the length of the trust term, specific provisions in the trust agreement, or the relationship of the assets to the grantor or the beneficiaries all can mandate a deviation from the duty to diversify.
- Notwithstanding the first conclusion, case law indicates that, once having decided that diversification is inappropriate in a particular case, a trustee should always communicate this conclusion to cotrustees, if any, and to all beneficiaries (both current and remainder). This is not a legal requirement but rather a "best practice" that a trustee ignores at her peril.
- If, after communicating this position, the trustee receives a complaint from any beneficiary, the trustee should take steps to remedy the problem rather than simply relying upon the consent of others or language in the trust agreement as a shield. The best possible course in this case is to seek instructions from the court having appropriate jurisdiction that the investment plan is correct and does not violate the trustee's duty to diversify.

- Even if the trustee receives no complaints, she should continue to "check in" with the beneficiaries (perhaps annually) and reconfirm the investment strategy, along with the fact that the trustee is not diversifying investments.
- Any trustee who has decided that the trust agreement requires, or the facts indicate, that the trustee hold a concentrated position should not stop the analysis there but rather should consider whether some hedging technique like a collar is available and appropriate. If the trustee believes such a technique should be considered, she should communicate the proposal to all beneficiaries before undertaking it and seek their approval or the approval of the court before proceeding.

These conclusions can appear to be nothing more than common sense; however, the case law indicates that following such procedures can keep a trustee out of trouble or at a minimum help her obtain summary judgment if she is sued by beneficiaries for her investment strategies.

Appendix A

Sample Trust Investment Language

The following sample language is intended purely as a starting point; changes in state law and the client's particular needs will dictate a more specific approach. Obviously, each of the exceptions is intended to be considered separately, depending upon the particular circumstances. Also, note that the indemnification language at the end should be considered whenever any of the exceptions is being used.

Trust Investments. The Trustee shall hold and invest trust assets pursuant to the **[STATE]** Uniform Prudent Investor Act (the Act), but with the following exceptions:

1. The Grantor has created this trust for the primary purpose of maintaining an interest in **[NAME OF CLOSELY HELD BUSINESS]**, or any successor entity thereto, and to preserve that interest for future generations. In keeping with this intent, the Trustee is directed to hold any interest in **[NAME OF CLOSELY HELD BUSINESS]**, or any successor entity thereto, and shall not be under any duty to sell such interest in order to diversify investments. The Trustee is directed to hold such interest whether or not it is productive of income **[WARNING: THIS SENTENCE IS INCONSISTENT WITH MARITAL DEDUCTION QUALIFICATION]**. The Trustee may dispose of such interest only with the consent of **[LIST CONSENTING PARTIES: BENEFICIARIES, TRUST PROTECTOR, KEY EMPLOYEES, ETC.]**.
2. The Grantor has created this trust for the primary purpose of maintaining an interest in **[IDENTIFY REAL ESTATE HOLDING]** and to preserve that interest for future generations. In keeping with this intent, the Trustee is directed to hold any interest in **[REAL ESTATE]** and shall not be under any duty to sell such interest in order to diversify investments. The Trustee is directed to hold such interest whether or not it is productive of income and regardless of the cost of maintaining such

interest **[WARNING: THIS SENTENCE IS INCONSISTENT WITH MARITAL DEDUCTION QUALIFICATION]**. The Trustee is further directed to follow the Development Plan, attached as Exhibit A to this Agreement, with respect to such interest and to use trust assets in whatever manner necessary to implement that Development Plan. **[THIS SENTENCE IS TO BE USED FOR REAL ESTATE DEVELOPERS THAT INTEND FOR PROPERTY TO BE USED IN A CERTAIN MANNER AFTER THE DEVELOPER'S DEATH AND REQUIRES THE CUSTOM DRAFTING OF A DEVELOPMENT PLAN, NOT INCLUDED HERE .]** The Trustee may dispose of such interest only with the consent of **[LIST CONSENTING PARTIES: BENEFICIARIES, TRUST PROTECTOR, ETC.]**.

3. The Grantor intends to fund this trust with a concentrated holding in **[NAME OF PUBLICLY TRADED SECURITY, MUTUAL FUND, OR INVESTMENT SECTOR]**. The Grantor recognizes that maintaining such a concentrated position is inconsistent with the provisions of the Act. In keeping with this intent, the Trustee is directed to hold such interest and may dispose of such interest only with the consent of **[LIST CONSENTING PARTIES: BENEFICIARIES, TRUST PROTECTOR]**.
4. The Grantor intends for the Trustee to seek the advice of the Grantor's financial advisor, **[NAME]**. In keeping with such intent, the Grantor hereby directs the Trustee to engage **[NAME]** to provide investment advice to the Trustee and to follow such advice, regardless of any provisions in the Act to the contrary.
5. The Grantor recognizes, in following the preceding directions, that the Trustee may have to administer the trust in a manner that is otherwise inconsistent with the provisions of the Act. The Grantor hereby releases the Trustee from any liability for following such directions and holds harmless the Trustee and the Trustee's successors and assigns from any such liability.

Appendix B

Investment Plan Flow Chart

What follows is a flow chart designed to assist the trustee or investment professional in determining the investment parameters for a given trust.

1. Trust Review.
    a. Does the Agreement contain any "intent" language? If yes, what is the grantor's purpose in creating the trust?
    b. Does the Agreement contain any language regarding investments?
        i. If yes, does the Agreement "direct" the trustee with respect to particular investments or merely "authorize" them?
        ii. If the Agreement merely "authorizes" investments, consider obtaining beneficiary approval or court instructions to follow such instructions.

2. Beneficiary Information.
    a. Does the Agreement spell out who are the "primary" beneficiaries (that is, those beneficiaries whose interests and needs are to be considered above others)?
    b. Does the Agreement require that, in making distribution decisions, a beneficiary's other assets and resources are to be considered?
    c. Does the Agreement define any beneficiary's interest in terms of "income"? If yes, consider annual adjustment between principal and income or conversion to a unitrust.
    d. Are there any actual conflicts among beneficiaries?

3. Transfer Tax Issues.
    a. Is the Trust exempt from generation-skipping transfer (GST) taxes?
    b. Will Trust assets be included in a beneficiary's estate, either because the trust qualified for a marital deduction or because a beneficiary holds a general power of appointment?
    c. Are there any other trusts created by the grantor or the grantor's family that have different tax consequences (for example, GST exempt or nonexempt, subject or not subject to estate taxes at a beneficiary's death, etc.)?

4. Special Assets. Regardless of any specific language in the trust agreement, are there any trust assets that have a special relationship to the grantor or the grantor's family, such that those assets should be maintained regardless of the duty to diversify? If yes, consider obtaining beneficiary approval or court instructions to follow such instructions.
5. Investment Strategy. In light of the preceding answers, complete the following:
   a. The time horizon of the trust is: ______________________.
   b. The primary beneficiary (if known) is: ______________________.
   c. The current cash outflow estimate is: ______________________.
   d. The trust will/will not be subject to estate or GST tax on distribution or termination.
   e. When developing the strategy, the following assets must be considered as part of the investment mix, due to a special relationship to the family:

      ____

      ____

      ____

Index

R

S

T

U

V

W